The gods of Creation

Analysing and Activating the Power of the Creative Mind

Paul Taiwo

ISBN:

978-0-6485465-0-4 (E-book)

978-0-6485465-2-8 (Paperback)

978-0-6485465-1-1 (Hardback)

Website: www.paultaiwo.com

DEDICATION

To everyone who works to create a better world.

ACKNOWLEDGEMENTS

I am thankful to God for the gift of life, time, and for inspiring me to write this book. You are the source of all creativity. All existence comes from You, and there is no reality apart from You.

Juliana Taiwo, my beloved wife, my queen—you've stayed with me through the good times and the bad. It is my privilege to be your partner. I will be forever grateful for your support, input, sacrifice, and feedback throughout the process of writing this book. You made this book a reality.

Adetoke and Adetola Taiwo, my treasured daughters, you keep me laughing. You are my reason for pursuing higher goals in life. I live to create a better world for you both.

My eternal gratitude to my parents, Pastor Simeon and Mrs. Grace Taiwo, who instilled Christian ethics in me. You both are models of resilience and strong leadership, and I have always admired your strength. You made me believe in myself. Thank you for your sacrifice and your prayers.

To my siblings – Adeleke, Adedeji, Victoria, Adedayo, and Aduragbemi Taiwo – I always felt safe and loved growing up with you. I know I can always count on you.

Thanks to Sam Adetiran, my brilliant editor who expertly polished my text and made this book the finished product it is today. I'm indebted to you for your hard work and excellence. Without you, this book might not have seen the light of day.

Yohana Akang, you're a dear friend and protégé. Thanks for listening for hours while I discussed this book with you. You were the first recipient of this masterpiece and I am grateful that you allowed me to share my thoughts in their raw form.

To Samuel Ekundayo—The Purpose Preacher—your writers' boot camp was impactful. Thank you for sharing your knowledge about writing. You are a major reason behind the success of this book. Thank you also for recommending Sam Adetiran—his help proved invaluable. God bless you.

CONTENTS

WHY I WROTE THIS BOOK

This book is all about God's ideal for creation. It is a book that helps you understand your God-given creative intelligence. It's easy to read because anything that is complex can be a bit hard to apply. It's also practical, which means it will provide you with pragmatic ideas that can be applied to your life to get results. Finally, it's a guide, meaning that it's just a skeleton that you can add flesh to. It doesn't give you everything, it's just a guide. It emphasises that our intelligence is God-given. We must always appreciate the fact that God is the giver of knowledge, wisdom, and understanding, and He's the One that gives us the power and that power means the intelligence to get wealth, to work. So, everything comes from God. It doesn't come from humans. So, even though we are creative gods, gods with a 'g'; we have a boss up there (in heaven) that dispenses knowledge and creativity. This book stresses creative intelligence. There are other forms of intelligence e.g. emotional intelligence, analytical intelligence, cognitive or memory, etc. This creative Intelligence talks about bringing something out of your inner being to this physical world. Here, I am referring to idea generation, and building institutions and things. I wrote this book for seven reasons (For three major reasons in particular)

The first reason is that I had an encounter with my boss. I have had cause to keep recounting that experience. My boss is a very kind-hearted man. Very supportive! I started working with him through the first job I got when I moved from the Middle East to Australia. My boss was very supportive and nice, but he wasn't a believer in God. He doesn't believe God exists. He's an atheist and self-proclaimed man. He is very good at his job and very competent. So, one day we got into a conversation, just a normal conversation because we had actually developed a good relationship, hence we could talk freely. During that conversation, he made a particular comment (I can't remember what exactly he said), and I just blurted out the statement, '*Thank God*', without giving it a thought. I knew he was an atheist, but sometimes you just say something without even being conscious of it. Of course, he heard me and said, '*Don't tell me you believe in God*'. I said I believe in God. He responded, '*Paul, you are too smart to believe in God, it's only fools that believe in God.*' I used that opportunity to tell him that I wasn't only a believer in God, I was also a Christian. Of course, the conversation went on and on. But one thing that shocked me was that attitude that Christians are supposed to be silly. I don't know why, but probably because of how we had comported ourselves in the last couple of years which has made people believe that you cannot be intelligent and be a Christian. It was shocking for me because from Africa where I came, Christianity was in vogue. It just never occurred to me that the label of not being intelligent can be attached to a Christian. It just wasn't part of my experience. We were proud to be Christians. So, when my boss mentioned that, I started to wonder what happened to Christianity in the western world that peddles the impression that losers will eventually succumb to religion. So, I set out to write this book to counteract that mindset. It is not correct. As Christians, we can be creative. We can be excellent. We can be leaders. We can be shakers and movers in society. We can do so much.

Secondly, when I was in medical school, I was very active in fellowship. I was the head of the technical department in my fellowship, then I rose to become the coordinator of the Christian fellowship, or what we call the president or the pastor of the institution's fellowship. So, in leadership, I was exposed to a couple of things in terms of people's lives and people's performance in their academics. Some Christians did very well, but the majority were average, including the ones I led in my fellowship. Then, some failed. They were very active in fellowship, but they failed. They had to withdraw from the institution as a result. They couldn't complete their studies. So, being someone who reflects a lot, and as a leader, I didn't like that outcome. I didn't want any of my followers to fail. How come they fail? Some of them had to repeat certain courses over and over again, and I didn't like that. Of course, a few people did well in terms of excellence. So, I began to ponder on what was happening. I thought as Christians we had a sound mind and we were created in the image of God, so what was the missing point here? Also, while I was in medical school, I noticed that when the best student in a class was a Christian, the fellowship or the Christian group that the person attends, or is part of, would just increase in size. Let's say that the best student in the place attracts an increased number of friends. That means that people are drawn to success. People are drawn to excellence and distinction. So, without even the fellowship preaching or going on evangelism or any campaign for Jesus Christ, people just came in there simply because the best person in their class was a Christian that attended their gathering. I also noticed that when the best student was a Muslim, there was an increase in Islamic activities on campus. It's just automatic. So, when the best person is a Christian, you see increased Christian activities, programmes, seminars, etc. But, on the other hand, when the best guy or the best student is a Muslim, you just begin to see increased Islamic activities without any effort. People are drawn to intelligence and creativity. So, this book was written to address this issue; to see why just only a few Christians excel. We will be looking at how we can use our success in life, especially in the secular space, to draw people to God without even opening the Bible.

Thirdly, the backwardness in Africa worries me. I've always been worried about this, even from my secondary school days. I do not mean to cast aspersion on any one or a sect of people. Africa is a deeply religious place, whether traditional religion, Christianity, or Islam. But, it is on the continent of Africa that you find the highest rate of poverty, disease, and all sorts of things. That is conflicting. If you have a people that are worshipping at least one god, either following Jesus Christ or following Prophet Muhammed, but their lives are not better off compared to people that say there is no God; what is the missing link? I was reading an article about intelligence, about how things came into existence. Scientists have worked and worked, but have not found any gene that codes for intelligence. They're still working on it. But, there's no validated study or validated research that explains why white people, the Caucasians, appear to be smarter than people of other colours. There are three races in this world, majorly. Broadly speaking, we have the Caucasians, Negroids (blacks), and the Mongoloids. The Caucasians have done so much in terms of development, creativity, science, technology, innovations, going to space, etc. Unless we want to deceive ourselves, the results are there for everybody to see. And everything is driven by their inventions and discoveries. Then the Mongoloids (Chinese, Japanese, etc.) have excelled one way or the other. However, the Negroids are always at the back and always catching up later. It worries me, yes it does. Of course, a few black people are doing great things. For example, blacks are doing great things in NASA, but as a race, we have not been able to do so much for ourselves. We receive the highest forms of donations. Everybody donates to Africa. We are always on the receiving end, and hardly giving back. We have contributed, but not in a very significant way. It worries me, but now, you find the concept of religion in Africa. So, how come? So, no gene says that Caucasians are better or are more intelligent than Negroids. There's nothing that has proven that scientifically. The Negroids have religion, but our religion has not helped us. So, this book has been written with the black race in mind, especially the Christians or blacks who are Christians, to address black backwardness in Africa.

Fourthly, this book is also written for those people who want to excel outside the four walls of the church. So, we have what I call the principle of *Applied Christianity* which explains that whatever you learn in the church can be applied in the marketplace. And it's not just about living a holy life, you can learn something in the church and apply it to science. I'm not talking about being a good person or a nice person. We know that everybody should be nice. But, you can apply the knowledge you gain from the Bible to Biology, Chemistry, Law, Engineering, Information Technology (E.g. You can learn something in the Bible that can help you develop something, like another form of a computer), etc.

This book was also written to address creative intelligence and transformational leadership, which makes the fifth and sixth reasons.

Finally, I wrote this book to address the insults poured on clergymen. I have been touched by these insults because, though I am a Doctor and a scientist in a way, I also came from a deeply religious background. My grandmother was the first person that left African religion for Christianity in my family. My dad was a part-time pastor who was working as a teacher. So, I have people around me who were religious but still worked in the secular world. I noticed that sometimes around 2010 and upward, there were a lot of insults thrown at pastors that they always want money. Pastors themselves may have contributed to that, maybe the way they've preached their messages focusing on money and how they can grab from people. Well, fine, but that doesn't give people the right to just insult them. I have written this book for pastors to see how they can be creative. You can be a pastor and develop a product. You can be a pastor and write computer programs. You can be a pastor and be a scientist. You can be a pastor and be a geologist. You can be a pastor and be an inventor. This way, you won't even have to go and ask people for tithe and offering. Through your creativity, you can become the highest giver in your church. I want to be the highest giver in a church I'd lead. Not that I would be waiting for people to pay tithes or offerings, I want to be the highest giver by my creativity through what I bring to the market, maybe I will invent something. And we should be able to invent because we have a background of that in the Bible. Going through the Old Testament, people that were involved in the secular world were religious. They were indispensable. They were excellent. So, this book is written for clergymen who want to be creative to bring something to the secular world, a product or service, at the same time, maintaining dignity and honour. This will ensure that nobody manipulates others because now, people are using money to control others. These people think that once they can give to pastors, they can control what they would say on the pulpit. Something like that should stop. Pastors should be able to get into that creative space too.

INTRODUCTION

Creativity occurs in five steps. From Genesis chapter 1 (the story of creation) we saw it recorded that, several times, God spoke and it came to pass. One would probably have the mindset that God just spoke and everything came into being. That is correct. But that's not the full story; it was beyond speaking. Because if you go to chapter two of Genesis, it said *God formed*. If God spoke and things came into being, then he didn't have to form again. After He spoke, He had to go to work, He had to form with His hands. Hence, creativity occurs in five steps as follows:

1. Idea or intelligence of God
2. Imagination
3. Emotions
4. Speech
5. Action

How come five steps were collapsed into one that made it seem like God just spoke and everything came into being in an instant? Now, let's take idea to be step one, imagination step two, our emotions step three, speech step four, and action step five. So, if I count 1,

2, 3, 4, 5, you can follow me objectively while I count subjectively. If I speed up the counting to 1, 2, 3, 4, 5, 1, 2, 3, 4, 5 you can still follow me. But, just imagine that we can speed up the counting process to the speed of light, It now becomes 1, 2, 3, 4, 5, 1, 2, 3, 4, 5, 1, 2, 3, 4, 5... the process becomes so fast that it now appears to have been collapsed into one instead of five. This is a simple explanation of what happened at creation. The five processes occurred at the speed of light. God is not light, but He created light. He is fast, super-intelligent, and capable. Imagine a supercomputer working at a high speed. I'm not saying God is a supercomputer. I'm just trying to paint a picture. There's no way you can comprehend the processes that go on in a supercomputer. Don't even let us go there, even let's say a simple computer. You don't know how it works. You just input something and it comes back to you at once. But behind that prom, behind that screen, millions of processes are going on at hyper speed. So, what I am trying to achieve with this book is to slow down that fast process for you. Let's say God is too fast for us because He is a superpower. But we are not superpowers, we are human beings. Our minds are finite, and we can only hold on to just finite parameters per time. So, instead of 1, 2, 3, 4, 5, 1, 2, 3, 4, 5, 1, 2, 3, 4, 5..., we'd now slow it down to as much as we can; 1 to 2 to 3 to 4 to 5. Therefore, what we will be considering is the role that idea plays in creativity, the role that imagination plays in creativity, the role that emotion plays in creativity, the role that speech plays in creativity, and the roles that action plays in creativity. I believe that reading through this book will be a worthy investment of your time.

- Paul Taiwo

1

THE RESPONSIBILITY TO CREATE

Christians, generally human beings, have the responsibility to create, it is not just an ability that we have. If you see creativity as only an ability, then you know that you can do it. But if you also see it as a responsibility, what you are obligated to do, or what you must do, then you must be creative. And why is that? God said, *'Be fruitful and multiply, and have dominion.'* Be fruitful, not only in your body in terms of bearing children, but talking about creating things. Be fruitful, be creative, multiply what you have created, and then have the dominion. And that responsibility was given to human beings and other creatures of God. God gave that responsibility to animals. But for human beings, as a leader of God's creation, when you place that responsibility on yourself you begin to see it differently. Because leadership is all about taking responsibility. So, take up the responsibility to create a solution. Take up the responsibility to create the next supercomputer. Take up the responsibility to take human beings to Jupiter. Some people took it as the responsibility to take human beings to the moon. They took it as a personal responsibility to take human beings to the moon. Some people took it as their responsibility to build a nuclear weapon. Some people took it as their responsibility to create a submarine. Some people took it up as a responsibility to cure cancer. So, that charge, that responsibility has been given to human beings, but it has also been given to Christians in particular,

'God, who at various times and in various ways spoke in times past to the fathers by the prophets, has in these last days spoken to us by His son, whom He has appointed heir of all things, through whom also He made the worlds.'[1]

---

[1] Hebrews 1:1-2 NKJV

Jesus Christ was the person that created the world, as seen in the above text. God made the world through Jesus Christ. So, when you say you are acting through someone, or I'm acting through you, you are the one doing it. I'm just staying in the background. I may give you the template or give you the instruction, but you are the one who does the work. As Christians, we can do greater works than Jesus did. So, apart from healing the sick or performing a miracle, what Jesus Christ did, we have the ability and the responsibility to also do. And because God created the world through Jesus Christ, we have the ability and the responsibility to recreate the world. So, when you take that responsibility, it changes everything for you. You begin to see yourself as a leader. You see yourself as a representative of God on earth. The misbehaviour that prevails among people, especially Christians is a result of a failure in taking this responsibility.

Secondly, because we are even created in the image of God, and God is an intelligent being who is brilliant and wise; there is no way our intelligence will match the intelligence of this God. And the bible says that we are created in the image and likeness of God[2]. So, we have the responsibility to project whatever His person

___

[2] Genesis 1:26-27

is. This is beyond holiness and being nice or being kind and merciful to people, although these are very very important. This projection also has to do with brilliance, a perfect intelligence, and genius that God exhibits. This is what we call the genius of Christianity.

Thirdly, we have the Holy Spirit indwelling us. 'And the Lord God formed man of the dust of the ground, and breathed into his nostrils the breath of life, and man became a living being'[3]. It means God downloaded His Spirit into us and we became a living being. So, man became a speaking being, or a living being, or an intelligent being, or a being that can imagine. When you say you have the Holy Spirit within you, what does it mean? That Holy Spirit is not only for speaking in tongues, and the Holy Spirit is not only for doing miracles. That Holy Spirit should come to bear in your secular work or study. That Holy Spirit should make you have the distinction. That Holy Spirit should help you to become the greatest inventor in this world. That Holy Spirit should make you become the greatest leader in this world. That Holy Spirit should make you become the most successful business owner in this world. That Holy Spirit should make you become the greatest biologist, greatest chemist, or the

---

[3] Genesis 2:7 NKJV

greatest anything you want to be. Of course, we are Christians and we want to go to heaven, but even while we are in this world, the Spirit of God in us should have an impact on our secular life.

'This is the history of the heavens and the earth when they were created, in the day that the LORD God made the earth and the heavens, before any plant of the field was in the earth and before any herb of the field had grown. For the LORD God had not caused it to rain on the earth, and there was no man to till the ground; but a mist went up from the earth and watered the whole face of the ground. And the LORD God formed man of the dust of the ground, and breathed into his nostrils the breath of life; and man became a living being. The LORD God planted a garden eastward in Eden, and there He put the man whom He had formed. And out of the ground the LORD God made every tree grow that is pleasant to the sight and good for food. The tree of life was also in the midst of the garden, and the tree of the knowledge of good and evil'[4]

Now, two trees were specified in the passage above, the tree of life, and the tree of knowledge of good and evil. But I want us to do something. I'm not desecrating

---

[4] Genesis 2:4-9 NKJV

the Bible, but just to make us understand it. Now, in your mind, instead of seeing two trees, picture three trees. So, the first of the three is the tree of life. The second one is the tree of good, and the third one is the tree of evil. Now, both evil and good are intertwined. This is why it was called the tree of life and the tree of knowledge of good and evil. The knowledge of good and evil are intertwined. Now, in the tree of life, I want us to see why this physical world is so important, why we must participate in this physical world as Christians, especially in the marketplace, especially in the secular world, why we must do well. The tree of life is that which is pure holiness, pure righteousness, talking about God Himself, talking about Jesus Christ. That which is spiritual, that is, which is perfectly spiritual. But the moment Adam and Eve ate from that tree of the knowledge of good and evil, we all ate with them. And in that way, we are all guilty of the fruit until Jesus Christ comes back. And let me tell you, let me explain it this way. This is why no one is righteous. So, you have the tree of life which is what I will also call the religious setting, service of God. But you have the tree of good, which is the secular world. That is where your knowledge of science comes in. Science is good, it is not evil, and is not spiritual. Geology, Accounting, IT, Astrology, Medicine, Chemistry, History, etc. they are all good. But they are also not spiritual and they are not evil. Because if they are evil, if you're a doctor then you have to be an evil person. It is good to be a doctor, so you must eat of the tree of good. Now, the other one is the tree of evil, talking about the satanic, occultic, or demonic world that we should run away from. We should participate in eating from the tree of life. We should separate the evil from the good and pick out the good to eat, talking about going to school. When you're going to school, when you're studying that course e.g. Veterinary Medicine, Law, etc. you are eating from the tree of good. And you separate what is demonic out of it. The tree of life and the tree of evil are battling to control the tree of good. That means that the spiritual world, God Himself is battling. Of course, He has won the battle. Satan is competing for the tree of good. He is competing with God to take over the tree of good. Satan is fighting to take over the legal system of the world, Information Technology (IT), Education, Media, Government, Military, etc. These things in themselves are not evil. But, Satan, the evil one, is trying to infuse evil into them. And that is where your responsibility as a Christian comes in, to align with God. You were created to be fruitful and aligned with God, to multiply and have a critical mass of people that should have dominion. There's something I call a critical mass. Critical mass or critical velocity is a critical value of anything you need to cause a change. If you say a critical mass of people, you need the minimum number of that, it can be 100 or it can be 50. The escape velocity or critical velocity is the minimum velocity you need to escape the gravitational pull of this world. So likewise, what the Bible is saying is that you should be fruitful, be creative, multiply until you have that critical mass, and then take control. So, this creative intelligence is not only about yourself, it is about strategic warfare. A strategic place in history. Eat with confidence from the tree of good because that is where creativity can be demonstrated.

2

IDEAS

Ideas rule the world. Ideas create control. Whoever can generate an idea and bring the idea from a concept to reality will eventually rule the world. This is what determines which country or what continent will lead the world. When you look at the great empires that ever existed, like the Egyptian empire, the Babylonian empire, the British empire, etc. they were all set up by ideas.

An idea is what somebody has that the other person doesn't have. It gives you an edge over another person. If you propose that you are going to improve the economy of Australia by $30 trillion, people will start taking you seriously. If you have the idea to achieve that, then you are in a very powerful place. Now as Christians, we have two sources of ideas. They are ideas from above, and idea from below. The ideas from the above refer to ideas from heaven and ideas from below refers to what is already in existence in this world. Going back to the Book of Genesis where God created the firmament, we observe that there was water above the firmament and water below the firmament[5]. So basically, what that means is that there's a complete world above the firmament. And the firmament is about time and space. The firmament itself is just time and space. Meaning there is a wealth of ideas above time and space, as well as below time and space, which is the physical world. Thus, what separates the heavens from the earth is time and space. Above that, we have ideas in the heavenly realms. That's why Paul said our blessings are in heavenly realms[6]. Part of those blessings is ideas. So those ideas are hanging in heaven and we also have ideas from below.

---

[5] Genesis 1:6-8

[6] Ephesians 1:3

IDEAS FROM BELOW

For this book, we are going to start with ideas from below. We will start from something simple, not big ideas that come from maybe your dreams or from the Holy Spirit. This is important because as Christians, we tend to complicate things or to over-spiritualise things and say we are waiting for God to give us an idea. That is very valid. But, we must start from the simple when you want to have an explanation for things. When you're trying to explain something, don't go for a more complex explanation, go for the simplest. So, we're going to start from something attainable, because we are in the world at the present and in the present moment, most of our activities are physical, not spiritual. Most people probably will not pray for more than one hour in a day, but you use twenty-three hours to do other things. In the story of the ladder Jacob saw at Bethel, the Bible stated that Jacob saw angels climbing up and coming down[7]. One would have expected that the Bible would say that the angels were coming down, then going up, because angels are spiritual beings and they are supposed to be in heaven. But the Bible said that the angels first ascended, then descended. Those beings are actually with us here. And ideas are actually with us here. There is an idea

---

[7] Genesis 12:28

that can go up climbing the ladder, but there's another idea that can flow from top-down. But when we are talking about ideas from below, we're talking about ideas that can go from down-up. Using Jacob's ladder to explain that; the angels had to go up first before coming down, so they were here. Now, the physical explains the spiritual, which means you cannot see the spiritual world, but you can see the physical world. So, we can understand God by understanding nature. You can understand God by understanding His created works because we can't see Him, but we can see everything that He has created. Hence, if you want to understand God in a way, you start from the works of His hand; physical things, that is the foundation of ideas from below.

How do you generate or receive godly, brilliant ideas from this physical world?

1. **Opportunities Around You**

What are the opportunities that are given to me? What are the opportunities I have around me that other people don't have? For instance, you may have the opportunity to study veterinary medicine at the University. God gave you that opportunity. There are billions of people that don't have the opportunity. We have around 6 to 7 billion people in the world. So, when you consider that probably just 1 million people out of that 7 billion have the opportunity to study that course, you realise that it was an opportunity you were given. Within that opportunity are thousands and thousands of ideas. Now let me say this first, if you are going to extract value and Ideas from that course, you must value that course (veterinary medicine). You can't hold it with a defective mindset or flimsy excuses. If you think about the fact that other people are studying law or medicine, or engineering, or that you didn't want to study that course in the first place; the ideas will not pop up. So, when you are going for your classes, whether an online or physical class, you should be asking if there is anything in that unit or lecture that you can translate to a business outside the university. You don't necessarily have to start now, because you still need to finish your degree. As they are teaching you, while other people are looking out for how to read and pass, you are looking at how to extract a business from the lecture. If your course is going to last for 5 years, for instance, you are pushing for how to become a Vet doctor if that's what you want to do, but you can also be looking out for how you can extract value from these things. It's no longer about just passing your exams. You consider how you can become a

Vet doctor and still be a business owner. If you like one of the animals that you treat for instance, you can create a business out of it. It doesn't even have to be a physical business, it can be you writing blogs, it can be you writing something that people want to know about animals. So, turn that cost or unit content; that subject you are studying now, into an idea. You can create a website for yourself now and start writing blogs. Start writing about what you do. Maybe you studied about the chimpanzee for instance, or you studied about rabbits during a lecture, you can study about other rabbits, and look at how you can extract value, the same way of extracting value from the Bible, to make it realistic and practical for people to live a good life. You can take any knowledge, it can be a story about rabbits, the quality of rabbits, the strength of rabbits, or how people can utilise the wisdom of rabbits for their lives. Start reading about it. Though you are still working on a doctorate, maybe for the next five years, by the time you have a blog or a website for five years, and you put in knowledge and trust to apply what you've learned here and translate it to another field. By the time you get to that point, you'll be an expert. So when you finish your Ph.D. or Masters, you will not be looking for a job again, you have created a business and people would begin to consult you. That is your opportunity. Don't just read and pass. Look at how you can extract value.

2. **Human Advice**

Human advice can be from your parents, your siblings, your friend, a mentor, or somebody that has done a business before. Somebody has to have been to where you've been or where you are trying to go before he or she can give you ideas. Such people can help you see what they got wrong that you should get right. There are business opportunities in listening to advice. Using the veterinary medicine business as an example again, you can pick up journals or publications about veterinary medicine. Things not even related to exams, you will see business opportunities. It doesn't even have to be a physical journal. It could be an online Journal of veterinary medicine USA or the UK. In those journals, they will talk about core scientific stuff, but they also talk about business. And you can turn that course or anything to a business opportunity. That's a form of human advice. It can be oral advice or written down. You need expert advice in the field you want to major in.

3. Nature

Now, I'm going to dwell more on this. I'm going to spend more time on this nature. If you're a student of nature, you will always rule nature, you will always lead people. Be fruitful, multiply, and have dominion is the mandate God has given you. This domination is not when you see an animal and step on it or when you see a plant and trample it. It's not about that. It's about understanding that animal or plant. Understanding is where education is very important. Understanding that animal or plant, that is, exposing their secrets, their internal world, and using it for your advantage and the advantage of humanity. That is what domination is all about. Domination is not oppression. To dominate something is to understand that thing to the extent that you have enough knowledge of that thing, it is not a mystery to you again. As Christians, we need to start thinking this way. Where do you think the submarine idea came from? Marine life. If you look at the basic design of a submarine, you will realise that it came from fishes. This is why Africans are lagging. We spiritualise things we see, everything is superstition. Anybody that can understand nature or any part of nature can use that understanding to build strength for himself or use it to lead other people or pressure other people. When you see a bat, what comes to your mind? Do you see like Africans see, *this is an evil bird*? Or do you see a bird you can understand and know how to create an airplane? Where do you think the idea of an airplane came from? From bats. So, it is only God that can create something from nothing. This is called *Ex Nihilo principle*. God created everything *Ex Nihilo*, something from nothing, after that, everything follows the law of cause and effect. As human beings, we don't have the power to create anything from nothing, but we have the power to use the law of cause and effect. The law of input and output. So, some people look at this and say, *'Oh, this is how we can create an airplane here'*. Study nature, be a student of nature. The study of nature is a tree of good, it is when you use it for evil intent that it becomes evil.

Let me give you another example. What about medicine? Medicine came from the medicinal value of plants. Some people thought that there must be something in certain plants that can be helpful, and they extracted the value. What about the computer? The computer came from the study of the human mind. A computer is just a physical representation or an adaptation, or a copycat, or an imitation of the human mind. Every internal process of the computer is the same internal process we find in the human brain. Your computer RAM (Random Access Memory), is an equivalent of a part in the human mind called short memory or short-term memory. Your screen or even your keyboard is equivalent to input like your eyes.

4. Formal Education

Now your formal education is related to what we already discussed about nature. You can find ideas in your academic books that you can translate.

5. Books

When you read, let's remove books that are not related to your study books, let's say you read a novel or read about sociology, anatomy, physics, economics, etc. as long as you There's a website called dummies.com. where you can understand any subject of interest. There is economics for dummies, engineering for dummies, and so on. This helps you to get the basic concepts in any field.

Once you can get a basic concept of any field, you can translate it to another field. So, when you're reading books, you're generating ideas.

6. History

The history of humankind is a wealth of ideas. Please, I encourage you to watch some movies on Netflix. Especially historical movies and documentaries. Of course, you have to pick the ones that are very clean because they also put all sorts of things, but just ignore those bad aspects like nudity and the rest. When you understand history, you can easily get ideas about what happened in the past and why. You can understand the needs of people 10 years, 20 years, or a thousand years ago and how they are different or connected to the needs of people now. You can see how their problems were solved that humanity has forgotten about today. You can also bring those solutions to the present time. History is very important. I watch movies maybe two or three times a month. Lately, the movie I'm watching on Netflix is, 'History 101'. And I recommend that to you. You will see how ideas are generated. It is a very popular movie. It is a series.

7. Past Experiences

These include successes and failures. Where have you succeeded or failed in the past? There are ideas locked up in our successes or failures. Everything is backed up by trial and error. We have to look at failure and say we can improve on these things. We can improve on the things that didn't work. Don't allow any failure to go without you learning something from it. The way you did it may have been wrong, but if you look at it closely, you will discover how to do it better.

8. Human needs around you

This is one of the most powerful sources of ideas. What are the needs of human beings around you? A lot of people started using the ZOOM application after the COVID-19 pandemic hit the whole world. I started using ZOOM in 2018. I immediately realised that it was a good platform for teaching, and I sent them a message as far back as 2018 for them to make a change because I wanted something more flexible. So, there was a need. What I did was that instead of just saying, solve this issue for me, I told them how to do it to get the result. I have also sent them another idea some months ago that if they do something, a lot of people are going to key into ZOOM. I let them know that if they apply my suggestion, especially for the religious people, they will see how things are going to turn out and nobody will be able to compete with them once they do it for religious people. What are the things that people need around you? What do you know that creates discomfort for people? Everybody wants comfort. So, what are the things we can do? What are the services and products you can develop to give people comfort in any area of their life? For instance, Western Union money transfer came about as a result of a need; the need to transfer money. Before then, people abroad send money to their loved ones, but it could take 30 days before the person gets paid. It was a laborious process for people to redeem monies sent to them. But people often need these monies quickly. This was how Western Union came to the rescue. It came as a response to the need for speed and comfort. What about the telephone? It came as a response to the need to communicate. Now, I want you to do something for me. Go online and type *Basic human needs* on Google, whatever you see there, write the list down. Take that list to God and ask Him to give you an idea that can solve at least one problem in at least one of the categories. Ask Him for one idea that can solve at least one problem in this category. The answer may not come now, but the answer will eventually come because there's always a need. There's always a problem to solve.

9. The time of crisis

This is the time for the most powerful ideas to be born - when there is a personal crisis, community crisis, or global crisis. The same thing that kills millions of people also creates wealth for some people. Crises put money in the accounts of some people, some people benefited from the wars. Also, people are benefiting from COVID-19. And I'm not talking from the evil kind of benefiting point of view, I'm talking about people who can create a solution. ZOOM, as I mentioned earlier, is benefiting from COVID-19. A health crisis is an opportunity to generate health products, an economic crisis is an opportunity to generate economic products, a geological crisis is an opportunity to generate geological products that can solve the geological issues. Power crisis or political crisis is an opportunity to generate political ideas or political solutions. Joseph's idea of saving 20% of the produce of Egypt during the 7 years of plenty[8] was an economic idea that solved an economic problem. Jacob's crossbreeding[9] was an idea to solve a personal crisis.

10. **The inventions of others**.

What other people have done can generate ideas. It is not about plagiarism or copying others and all that, but you can look at what other people are doing. If somebody builds a computer, you look into that computer and ask yourself, how can I copy this computer and improve on it? That is how, right now, China rose to power. I'm not interested in other people's ideas but what China did was just to copy everything everybody is doing, and mass produce it. They were not strong enough economically, educationally to start generating their ideas. They are also different 50 years after World War 2 because they were just copycats, but now they are generating their noble ideas.

---

[8] Genesis 41:34
[9] Genesis 30:37-39

You can get ideas from the criticisms of the inventions of others by reading through the reviews under a product you desire to purchase or have purchased e.g. a book or mug you bought on Amazon. The bad comments usually reflect the needs and expectations of the people.

11. Criticism

What are the inventions of others that people criticise? when people say bad things about you, don't be hurt about it, see it as an opportunity for self-improvement. Don't even be hurt about it. Don't be bitter. Go to the comment of that person and see if what this person is saying is bad enough. Is there anything good that you can bring out from it? There are benefits in good comments as well as bad comments.

12. Government policies

See, the government will always change policies. They love their wealth. The government can go back and make a policy that will change everything. You can start a restaurant business that is booming, and they go ahead to make a policy that will drop traffic from that business, but people being driven away from that business is an opportunity for the business. Be flexible. Flexible people want to get the best out of life. You know, even scientists sometimes modify theories that are not working.

13. Trends and countertrends

Trends mean what is in vogue. What is in vogue are those things people are willing to pay for now, at this moment. People are willing to pay for ZOOM so they can have meetings one-on-one. What is in vogue is what people are willing to pay for to enjoy. So, look at it, what are people willing to pay for? What are people proud to wear? What kind of clothes do people pay for? What kind of food are people proud to eat? That is what is called a trend. Which sector of the economy or which sector of my field is the money going into?

We also have counter-trends. Now, this ZOOM thing is not going to go on forever, it is a trend now. By the next 20 years, if they're not very careful, it may no longer be a trend.

IDEAS FROM ABOVE

This one is about what comes from above; the manna from above. Since we know that manna comes from above, you should also know that food grows from the ground. When you plant maize, cassava, etc, they all grow from the ground, isn't it? Manna comes from above, but there's an unforgettable thing about Manna; it doesn't always last (like the Bible showed us) God expects us to engage with this earthly, physical realm. Thus, for continuity, there's a pattern in this regard. Therefore, ideas that come from above are divine, they are God-given and are supernatural.

Now, I'm going to move from simple to complex. This is because once you take life from simple to complex, it becomes easy to become masters, professionals, or maybe experts in fundamentals. So, there's a need to take life from the fundamental to the complex. Idea from above doesn't take a lot of stress for manifestation, its output happens at ease. This is the reason why two persons will be exposed to an experiment, and one person will demand a lot of constant practice before attaining to what looks like perfection while the other gives excellent output with little or no stress; everything the later does, works perfectly. You can even get enough ideas from below, for anybody who is not a Christian.

HOW TO RECEIVE IDEAS FROM ABOVE

1. Sermon

For persons who are Christians, the number one way of receiving ideas from above is through a sermon. The church is not only about social interaction, preaching, preacher's interaction, fellowship, prayer and fasting, and other things. Nevertheless, if someone is preaching, you, as a person listening to that preaching, should shift your mindset that this is like listening to a lecture. Of course, a sermon should be enjoyable and impactful, but a sermon is also an instruction. It all boils down to mindset. For instance, an average sermon which is a form of a lecture will last about 45 minutes. An average lecture lasts for about 30 to 45 minutes in the university. Now, a sermon shouldn't only teach you about spiritual things like holiness and all those sorts of things, a sermon should also teach you about life. This is because someone may be thinking of taking a personal decision about life based on what somebody is preaching. For instance, based on what someone preached in the past, I got an idea, implemented it, and I got results. So, whenever we're listening to someone, a recorded sermon, or live streaming on YouTube, look beyond the spiritual undertone to see how you can adapt it. Consequently, we are looking at concepts in the sermon that can be translated into concepts in the marketplace. Just the same way we can translate concepts from the marketplace into a sermon in the church, you can do vice versa. A sermon is very strong, especially when the pastor is knowledgeable. Pastors should be knowledgeable, I believe they should read wide.

2. Logos

Logos means the Word of God as it appears, as written. When you take this approach in reading the Bible, you can never get bored of reading the Bible. Let's assume you are trying to memorise something in the Bible, especially when we're reading a story to see how people behaved in the Bible, not even attaching any spiritual meaning to it, we can take the story of how people behaved in the Bible and apply that wisdom in our workplace or to our study. For instance, let's say you are trying to study how animal breeds, you can take the story of Jacob when he was with Laban rearing his livestock, and find out how to adapt it to what you are doing. You can adapt it at a conceptual level, or a real level. You can now say that if I have a business, and I'm trying to do this, I may not do the same thing

Jacob did, but I'm going to do something similar. I'm going to look into it and unlock it. When you read the Bible this way, It will never be boring. This is because you are trying to feed your secular life, and the secular life feeds you back. Okay, let's take memorising the group two elements of the Periodic table that's below the hydrogen. The next one is lithium, then beryllium, etc. When you're trying to memorise these elements, because you're a Christian, you already know all the names in the Bible. The names in the Bible are familiar to you. Because now you do for someone who's not a Christian you have names you have concepts in the Bible. You can use concepts in the bible that you are already familiar with to remember things. E.g. When you are remembering holiness, you're remembering hydrogen, so you don't have to go back and study holiness again. Once you can blend the spiritual with the physical and everything becomes the same to you, memorising will be easy. This is because you're not going to struggle to remember some names in the Bible like that of Laban, neither will you struggle to remember the name of Jacob or Jesus? No.

So with logos; you take the Word, study, and adapt it. Adapt stories in the Bible, adapt the names in the Bible, adapt the numbers in the Bible. E.g. You can use the 24 elders to remember 24 elements in the periodic table. So you are benefiting. We are not saying that those elders are elements, neither are we saying they are equal or equivalent, but we are saying that they are similar. Similar concept, but not equivalent.

3. Revelation

This revelation or rhema is the domain of God. The domain is what is called 'The Eureka Moment'. It is the prerogative of God. Revelation is beyond making an analogy, it is an act of God unlocking a secret. For instance, anyone can read a similar story in the Bible with you, but may not have the same understanding, interpretation, or revelation of that story. The first one was about logos; logos can be applied by anybody, but revelation is something that God gives you at a moment to explain a story in the bible or a bible passage. Some other people may read the same story or passage and be completely blind to it. Note that revelation must not be inside the church only, it can be anywhere. You can read the parables of Jesus Christ. For instance, the parable of Jesus Christ about the servants that were given five talents, two talents, and one talent[10]. You can read that story, get revelation, and determine within your business who you are going to give five responsibilities to and who you're going to give two or one, and how you're going to punish the

---

[10] Mathew 25:14-30

one that is not productive. Revelation comes in when God wants to unlock a deeper meaning. You can read logos and apply it to your everyday life, but you can also read that logos and God will unlock a deeper meaning that you alone will have. Revelation is specific and unique

4. Voice of the Holy Spirit

The Holy Spirit is like a partner. If you place the Holy Spirit to explain some things to you, not only the things in the Bible, but things of nature, the things about chemistry, physics, and biology, or the periodic table, the Holy Spirit will explain it to you. The Holy Spirit's explanation is not bound to just what you read in the Bible, because everything is created by God. The knowledge of geology, astronomy, biology, or anything we learn in school is not outside God. They are within God and can be found in the Bible. Consequently, the Holy Spirit is a representative of God at the moment, so, place a demand on the Holy Spirit. How do you recognise the voice of the Holy Spirit? The Holy Spirit is just a real partner that can help you solve problems. Assuming you have a problem in your workplace, go to the Holy Spirit and ask Him what to do. The Holy Spirit can come as an inner voice.

5. Human Spirit

Of course, it is good to hear from the Holy Spirit, but because your spirit has been regenerated, your spirit can tell you what to do, regarding the activities of your everyday life. How do you know that? Human beings are a combination of spirit, soul, and body. Within the soul, we have the mind, the will, and intellect. But within the human spirit, we have three things there. We have love, intuition, and light. These things can be understood. A human being is exactly the combination of light, pure lights. That's why the Bible says that 'God is light, and in Him is no darkness at all[11]. God said, 'let us create man in our image'. Talking about the spirit man, the spirit man is the image of God which is pure light and pure love, because God is love. The other aspect is Intuition. Intuition is a Knowing, a perception, something you may not be able to explain. When you have that kind of feeling, don't let it go away, don't think, just write it down. You may not act on it, but try to understand why you are perceiving that thing or why such intuition is coming to you. Note that this intuition may be positive, negative, or maybe solution-driven, that is, solution-focused. For instance, maybe you're trying to build something, perhaps a house, and an engineering issue pops up, you can

---

[11] 1 John 1:5

perceive the solution from your spirit. Of course, that also has to do with your body of knowledge, that is, whether the person has read very well on the subject matter. That is the human spirit.

6. Word of Knowledge

Okay, this one is basically for Christians. This is part of the gifts of the Spirit. The gifts of the Spirit are meant to help us to live a normal human life. They are not for what people use in knowing bad things about people. No, that is the spirit of paranoia. I've told somebody before, if you say that you have a Word of Knowledge and that Word of Knowledge has not helped you to solve a problem in your own life, then it's not Word of Knowledge, it is a word of paranoia or just a suspicious spirit. The Word of Knowledge is solution-focused. I can give you several examples in the Bible. For instance, When the Syrian army was attacking Israel's army, Elisha will sit in his room to receive 'Word of Knowledge' and know what they (the enemies) were planning[12]. In other words, the Word of Knowledge can tell you about what has happened in the past, or what is happening now. It doesn't necessarily give you the solution, but it makes you understand it. Another instance about Word of Knowledge was when

---

[12] 2 Kings 6:9

Naaman a leprous man, was told by Elisha to go and wash in the Jordan river seven times[13]. That wasn't a performance of a miracle, because the performance of a miracle would have involved Elisha touching him. Rather, he told Naaman what to do and it solved a health problem. The instruction Elisha gave to Namaan wasn't a religious one. It was simply a solution to a problem. That is what Word of Knowledge is designed to do for you. You can always rely on the Holy Spirit when you don't know what to do. During the season I was writing this book, I had a lot to do. As a doctor, I had things to read up, and exams to prepare for. My schedule was very demanding that I needed time for reading. I usually had a discussion meeting every Friday night between 9 p.m. and 12 a.m. I discovered that my adrenaline was always high after that meeting, so the Holy Spirit inspired me to leverage that adrenaline and convert the time immediately after the meeting to reading time. This helps me to read for six hours between 12 a.m. and 6 a.m every Friday into Saturday.

Another example of the Word of Knowledge in the Bible was where before Paul set out on a journey by the sea with other men, he said, 'Men, *I perceive that this*

---

[13] 2 Kings 5:10

voyage will end with disaster and much loss...'[14] That is a Word of Knowledge. What was going to happen wasn't a religious activity, it was a natural event. A storm was coming, and somebody said that something was coming, it was a natural event. People think all these kinds of things are sometimes spiritual, but they are natural things, natural events. You can have a Word of Knowledge about the economy, about what the government is going to do, you can be warned ahead of time.

7. Word of Wisdom

The focus of the Word of Knowledge is to paint the picture (that is, give you a view) so that you can understand what is happening, but the Word of Wisdom must tell you what to do. The Word of Knowledge can tell you about the problem, to understand the problem, you may not necessarily have a solution. On the other hand, the Word of Wisdom is solution-driven. If there is no solution, there is no wisdom. if it doesn't contain a solution, then it is not a Word of Wisdom, because wisdom must be applied. Wisdom is always practical, wisdom is always pragmatic. For instance, let's say you are trying to crack a code in your workplace or your community, or

---

[14] Acts 27:10 NKJV

maybe you're trying to build a profitable business, the
Word of Wisdom will give you specifications on what
to do and it is usually one or two specific solutions.
What Daniel told Nebuchadnezzar was a Word of
Wisdom because he gave him a solution. Another
biblical example of the Word of Wisdom is the story of
Joseph and Pharaoh. What Joseph told Pharaoh is a
Word of Wisdom. It was Pharaoh that had the dream,
he saw an impending problem, the interpretation of
the dream was Word of Knowledge because it was a
problem that gave no solution. After the interpretation,
Joseph finally gave a solution. That is a Word of
Wisdom because it gave a solution. Word of
Knowledge will only paint a picture to you and give
you a good understanding of the problem, but that
doesn't mean you have a solution, but when you have
the solution, you now have the wisdom or wisdom
key. Note that the fact that you understand a problem
doesn't mean you must have the solution. This solution
can come in another bit, or God can put the two of them
together, both Word of Wisdom and Word of
Knowledge. Nonetheless, just make sure you
understand that when you have seen the problem, you
may not necessarily have the other - solution.
Solutions must be practical, it must be a to-do. In Word
of Wisdom, you must have a to-do list, that is, to have
what you're working with. Now, all these things must

be taken out of the church. Though of course, it is within the church, it must be extrapolated into the secular world. Wisdom now is not just about a preacher stopping during his sermon to give a word to somebody like, '*Somebody is sick here*' or '*Somebody just slept with another person here*'. It is beyond that. It must be applicable outside the church, like your workplace.

8. Prophecy

Prophecy tells you about the future. It's a prediction, a prediction of what is about to come. Prophecy is not limited to the second coming of our Lord Jesus Christ. When the prophets spoke in the Old Testament, they spoke about things that people can relate to like impending slavery, somebody about to die, etc. For instance, when a prophecy came that Hezekiah was going to die[15], it was a prediction of a health challenge. Prophecy can be a prediction of economic problems or economic growth, it doesn't have to be negative, it can be positive. So, pray to the Holy Spirit. The Gift of Prophecy doesn't have to be you saying '*Thus saith the Lord*' or '*God told me this thing*' There a lot of things that God will tell me that I will see, but I'll just say it normally like a normal conversation, the same way I will tell you or I will talk to a friend. You don't need to

---

[15] 2 Kings 20:1

say *'God said no'*, we know it is God and you have the
Holy Spirit. So, you can be given a prophecy that can
make you see what is about to come, in your career, in
your line of study, the Spirit of Prophecy can tell you
that in the next five years, the government will make a
policy that will make life easy or hard for you, that is
prophecy. In other words, prophecy will predict what
the government is about to do in the next five years,
Word of Knowledge will make you understand it
because the fact that somebody told you something
doesn't mean you understand it, then the Word of
Wisdom will place you in a position to either solve the
problem or cope with it, or find a way out.

9. Angelic Visitation

Angelic visitation shouldn't always be taken in the
context of religion alone. In the case of Balaam, an
angel appeared to him when he planned to go curse
the children of Israel and his donkey refused to move
because of the angel[16]. When an angel came to Mary,
it was about getting pregnant[17], it wasn't in the context
of the church. Thus, an angel can come to you but I
don't want us to get into that too much. This is because
we still need to live a normal life. Just know that an
angel can come to you, but be careful, don't go and seek

---

[16] Numbers 22:23-27
[17] Luke 1:30-31

angelic visitation. People that do that get into a lot of errors in life. Know that they exist, but don't pursue angelic experiences at all costs, it's not good.

10. Dream, Visions, and Trances

Your Dream may not necessarily be something you should get anxious about, but sometimes your dream can tell you about a lot of things. For instance, if you're trying to understand the concepts in your book after reading, solutions can come to you from your dream. I want to paint a picture of things that are easily relatable, not complex things. When you have a dream if you can remember it, fine. Try seeing how that dream relates to events around you, or predict events that are about to come but don't get too carried away by a dream. If you forget a dream, you don't get bothered about that.

11. Audible Voice

Again, it is possible to hear an audible voice. I don't want to dwell so much on this because of its psychological side. What the devil has done is that someone can be mad and claim he/she can hear voices. Despite this, I can tell you people have proven, even in this current age, that God can speak to people through an audible voice.

In conclusion, my advice is that you focus on the simple things that are easily reachable to you. A sermon is always present. When you have the time, you can listen to the sermon. For logos, you can read the Bible. The same goes for the Word of Knowledge, the Word of Wisdom, and Revelation, but for angelic visitation; a lot of people may not even see an angel until they die. Hence, focus on what is common. So when you put these things together; Ideas from below, and Ideas from above. They can be combined.

IDEAS AND GOD'S WILL

One of the common things among Christians as it has to do with ideas is what we call the will of God. Usually, we want to confirm our ideas. We want to be sure the idea is God's will for us and all of that. Of course, it's not everything good that is godly. It's not every good idea that is a godly idea. It is okay to confirm if an idea is from God or not. I don't have any issue with that. However, I have a bit of an issue with what people call the will of God. It sounds very religious. I have discovered in my private life that many times when we say we want to confirm if an idea is from God, we are covering up for something else. It may be born out of the fear to act, fear of the unknown, guilt, or a sense of insecurity. We usually are succumbing to the fear that the project before us will fail, so we try to get a 100 percent assurance from God that we will succeed. We need to be careful of overanalysing things to the extent that we are paralysed to take action or make decisions. It's alright to seek God's will, but not at the expense of taking initiative.

The best way to go about this is to say, *I want to seek the wisdom of God about this idea.* When we approach ideas with this disposition, we acknowledge that God is the originator of good ideas. The premise here is that as a mature born again Christian, the Holy Spirit indwells you, and as such, He is meant to influence every of your idea. So, your ideas are meant to be generated with the help of the Holy Spirit. Instead of asking God to tell you yes or no about your ideas, you should ask Him for more wisdom on how to go about the idea.

Most of the inventions we enjoy as Christians today; Microsoft, Telephone, Cars, etc. are a result of inventions from people who didn't need to specially ask God if they should invent those things. They just went ahead because they are solving a problem. On the other hand, we as Christians enjoy these inventions.

How To Know That An Idea Is a Godly Idea

1. Does the idea glorify God? You should be able to ask yourself, without going to God first, if the idea glorifies God or not.

2. Does it solve human problems? Usually, any idea that solves human problems is most likely to be a godly idea than not. God goes with anything that solves human problems. An invention that can solve HIV, ignorance, poverty, etc. is an idea that is worthy to be pursued.

3. Does it improve the human condition? If the idea gives comfort to humanity, raises the level of existence of humanity, then it is a godly idea.

4. Am I prepared for this? You need to ask yourself if you are competent enough, skilled enough, etc. to execute that idea.

5. Is it the right place and right time? Every idea has a right place and time of fulfillment.

6. Does this idea resonate with your spirit? Any idea that resonates with your spirit, in conjunction with the Holy Spirit, in the form of peace that passes all understanding is a godly idea. Note that this peace is not the absence of trouble or doubts.

Once again, doing the will of God is very important, but we must not use it as an excuse to feed our fears, inactions, and insecurities.

In the next chapter, we are going to start looking at Imagination. What we have considered in this chapter is to know how to receive an idea. Once you receive that idea, you must work with that idea. You must interpret that idea. It must be something vivid.

3

IMAGINATION

Why imagine?

Why do we have to use our faculty of imagination, especially as Christians? Many Christians believe that the Holy Spirit and Jesus Christ will just do everything for them. When we became Christians some of us just suspended our imagination and suspended our mind, but nobody can amount to anything in life without quality use of his mind, or his imagination. One of the pastors I respect said that we are not supposed to use our imagination. But I disagree respectfully with the person. I believe that we should use our imagination. It is a faculty that God gave to us. The first thing I want to do here is to disabuse your mind, in the sense of removing the sense of guilt surrounding imagination. Because one of the major things about Christianity is that sometimes, maybe because of the way we pass on the message, it is built on guilt, guilt surrounding sin, guilt surrounding condemnation, guilt surrounding punishment, and all that. We need to remove that veil surrounding imagination. I'm going to use the Bible a lot because this book is based on the Bible. I'm going to address the Bible verses that seemingly, on face value, say that we should not imagine, we should just trust the Holy Spirit and trust God and Jesus Christ. Then, I will go to the Bible verses that say that we should use our imagination, the faculty of our mind. Then I'll go to the Bible verse that resolves the two contradictions, one saying no and the other one saying yes, then I'll look at the ways to resolve the contradiction.

'For the weapons of our warfare are not carnal but mighty in God for pulling down strongholds, casting down arguments and every high thing that exalts itself against the knowledge of God, bringing every thought into captivity to the obedience of Christ, and being ready to punish all disobedience when your obedience is fulfilled'[18]

---

[18] 2 Corinthians 10: 4-6 NKJV

Some people have used this Bible verse above to say, 'Oh no! We should cast down imagination because some Bible translations say casting down imaginations. Some argue that it is a spiritual thing, we are supposed to be spiritual, the Holy Spirit should be the voice, which is correct. The Holy Spirit should be the voice guiding us, like our compass. As followers of Christ, we should follow the Holy Spirit. But, don't forget that human beings are essentially tripartite, that is we have three natures: we are spiritual, we are soulish, and we are physical. In the spirit of the man, we have love, intuition, and so on. In the soul, we have your mind, your imagination, etc. In the body, we have the brain or intellect which should synchronise with the soul and your soul should synchronise with your spirit. But some people believe we should just be spiritual and Christians can sometimes be hyper-spiritual, or excessively spiritual, or lacking the ability to recognise reality and participating in the physical world actively. And when I say participating, I'm talking about leadership, not just going to school, not just going to work, or studying a course. This is spiritual, you see your work, your university, your course as spiritual. So, on face value, this scripture above is saying that we should cast down all imaginations, cast down all arguments because they exalt themselves against the knowledge of God. The issue is that the imagination being referred to here exalts itself against the knowledge of God. I'm going to teach, through this book, how not to exalt imagination above the knowledge of God, when we look at the limitations and the pitfalls of imagination.

Another Bible verse that people quote to say that we are not supposed to imagine is the story of the Tower of Babel. 'And they said, "Come, let us build ourselves a city, and a tower whose top is in the heavens; let us make a name for ourselves, lest we be scattered abroad over the face of the whole earth." But the LORD came down to see the city and the tower the son of men built. The LORD came down to see the city and the tower which the son of men had built. **And the LORD said, "Indeed the people are one and they all have one language, and this is what they begin to do;** now nothing that they propose to do will be withheld from them. Come, let Us go down and there confuse their language, that they may not understand one another's speech."'[19]

God came down. Yeah, but the question is, Why did God come down? Imagine your nephew or your baby or my small daughter trying to build up a sandcastle.

---

[19] Genesis 11:4-7 NKJV

There's no way I'll be threatened by that sandcastle. I shouldn't be threatened if my daughter says she will build a sandcastle bigger than my house. If I do, then something must be wrong with me. Well, since God came down and stopped them from continuing, it means they were challenging the authority of God. God felt threatened, so to speak, and had to resort to confusing their speech. Because of this, some preachers have said, '*Oh, because God had to confuse their language at Babel, then we are not supposed to use our imagination*' That's one argument that people aren't used to.

Now, let us consider a case where God encouraged imagination. 'And the LORD said to Abram, after Lot had separated from him: "Lift your eyes now and look from the place where you are – northward, southward, eastward, and westward; for all the land which you see I give to you and your descendant forever."'[20]

Imagination is about lifting your gaze. That's figurative, I'm not talking about literal lifting of the eyes. Imagination is lifting your horizon, lifting your gifts, and your sights on a vision in life. In the Tower of Babel story, God said, '*No, you guys are not doing this, I will disrupt you guys*'. But in this case, God is

---

[20] Genesis 13:14-15

encouraging Abram, using the power of metaphor, to compare what He wanted to do so that Abram can grasp it because there was no other way to explain to him. He used the metaphor of the land that Abram could see to explain to him what imagination was about. At this point, Abram did not even have a child, yet God was assuring him in the next verse that his descendants will inherit the land. In another place, God assured that they will be as numerous as the sand. This was God encouraging man to imagine and go beyond the limits of his brain.

'And even as they did not like to retain God in their knowledge, God gave them over to a debased mind, to do those things which are not fitting;'[21]

The reason why God punished these sets of people referred to in the text above obviously wasn't that they had knowledge. God is not threatened by knowledge. He wants us to be knowledgeable. He even said my people perish for lack of knowledge[22]. So, He knows that knowledge is important. But the issue here is that they did not retain God. What does it mean not to retain God? It means they did not retain the authority of God. They wanted to make it easy for themselves to get and they wanted to raise themselves higher than

---

[21] Romans 1:28 NKJV
[22] Hosea 4:6

God. And God said, '*Oh no! I'm the boss*'. You can do the imagining. You can do the knowledge. You can do your science. You can do your physics. You can do your biology. But, your knowledge of value is still limited. Because there is no amount of discovery that can surpass God. You don't even know everything. So because these people did not retain God in their knowledge, God gave over their best minds to do those things which are not fitting or which are not right. So the issue is retention. You can read wide; study nature, study politics, study sociology, study anatomy, study anything you want to study. But, you must retain God. If that knowledge doesn't contradict the Word of God, what you are saying is that the Word of God takes the number one place. That's what it means to retain God. You get so used to continuing to do your secular job, both within your mind and your algorithm of decision making. You will say the Word of God exists and that's what it means to retain God in your knowledge, to retain the leadership and the authority of God in your knowledge.

GOD, THE ORIGINATOR OF IMAGINATION

God was the first person that exemplified imagination. 'Then God said, "Let Us make man in Our image, according to Our likeness; let them have dominion over the fish of the sea, over the birds of the air, and over every creeping thing that creeps on the earth"'[23]

God's imagination was at work here. He imagined what the man would be like. He had a picture in mind as He communicated with the Trinity. Imagination is not something outside of the Bible, we have an example in God. Imagination is when you see far ahead, to look at the quality, the future, the location, the characteristics of anything you want to do. In verse 26 of Genesis chapter 1, God had an idea – to create man, but in verse 27 the idea was implemented. We can see the step that God took. Now in terms of imagining, our imagination is a God-given cognitive faculty, which we must use. This means that as beings created in the image, likeness, and character of God, we must deploy our imagination the same way God did. I hope with these few points, I've been able to disabuse your mind about feeling guilty when you use your imagination.

WHAT IS IMAGINATION?

Imagination is a mental picture, a vivid mental representation, or an image from your mind, which is a prototype or a precursor of physical reality. It

---

[23] Genesis 1:26 NKJV

involves your mind, it must be engaged, and the Holy
Spirit cannot do this job for you. Jesus cannot do this
job for you. God cannot do it for you. You must involve
your mind. It's a mental thing, a representation. It's a
representation, it's not the real thing, but a shadow of
things to come. His image is now a prototype. What
does it mean to be a prototype? The first copy of
anything is the prototype. God made Jesus Christ and
then replicated Him in us. If you want to visit your
girlfriend today; naturally, automatically, without
even forcing it out, you see in your mind's eye what
will happen ahead; what you are going to do when you
meet her at the restaurant, how you will go buy
clothes, and if possible, how you will drive the car from
the garage to the house. That is imagination at work.
To imagine is to see. Imagination works the same way
your natural mind works. Imagination is close or
similar to the process of vision.

FEATURES OF IMAGINATION

It is flexible.
It is a work in progress and is not set on concrete. When
you begin to imagine, it is not fully formed. Things can
change. And when things change, don't feel guilty

about it. It is part of the process. It is developmental. You don't need to know everything at once.

It is intentional

In the sense that it requires making deliberate efforts. It is not something you do passively. Of course, some things will come to you without you getting involved, like inspiration, but to live a happy life, you must be intentional.

It is focused

You must be focused when it comes to imagination. It must be something you know that you are doing, it is not a dash or a sprint, it is a marathon.

It is fragmentary

Imagination to build anything worthwhile is fragmentary. It doesn't come as a whole. It comes in bits and pieces, in parts. Everything that you have to do, you have to know in parts. So, it's like putting a puzzle together; you could fix a piece today, another next week, and so on. Don't stress your mind. Like a giant pizza, you take it slice by slice, nobody can put 2 slices of pizza into the same mouth at once.

It is additive.

Additive in the sense that it is so massive, it usually comes in bits that can be added together. It is summative. So you put it, maybe you are reading something today. Certain events can add up to give you a full picture in your mind.

It is constructive

It is constructive in the sense that it's mostly positive. A positive thought will not lead you into anxiety or depression. Of course, it can put the responsibility on you, but it won't stress you. To be constructive means it is positive and innovative. Innovative means it can be something new or an improvement on the old.

It is productive.

What that means is that it results in the quality use of your time. While you go through the process of imagination, it will be worthwhile. That means that you're not losing because life is about opportunity costs. Imagination must make the best use of your time.

It is logical.

It must be intellectual. You must involve your mind. It must employ the power of deduction and induction. Deduction means when you look at a fact and extract something valuable. While induction means something that is already within you that you are bringing out. A deduction is from outside-in, while induction is inside-out. Induction is when you break a piece down into logical units, while deduction is when you put bits together in a logical way.

It is voluntary.
Voluntary in the sense that it mustn't be intrusive. It must be under your willpower. It is not something that intrudes into your mind or your daily activities. Imagination is voluntary. It is something you want to do, it is different from hallucination where thoughts come into your mind through some form of mind manipulation or distortion.

It simulates.
A simulator operates by what we call virtual reality. Virtual reality is imagination. It's like a mental imitation of what is real or a breathalyser. It is a dress rehearsal for something real.

It is stimulating
Both intellectually and emotionally, imagination is stimulating. When I say stimulating, it must make you wiser. Your IQ must increase. You must be more

knowledgeable. You must be better, and smarter. Your IQ, at least, must increase by that process of imagination. That's what it means for it to be intellectually stimulating. To be emotionally stimulating means that when you think about that thing, you will be happy. When we get to the emotional aspect of creation, I will explain more. It must be something you want to spend your time doing because it creates a sense of joy or pleasure within you. Any imagination that makes you depressed is not a good one. It doesn't come from God, and it's not productive. Anytime I'm preparing for a message, I feel happy because it stimulates me both intellectually and emotionally.

It must be comparative.
Comparative in the sense that imagination itself does not exist in a vacuum. It exists in the context of your society, in the context of your family, in the context of your community, in the context of your state, country, or race. Imagination is dependent on your memory; it is dependent on your past knowledge, past abilities, skills, achievements, or exposure. That is why it is comparative.

It must be solution-driven.

We have programmes all over the world. There will always be problems, hence there will always be a need for solutions. This imagination is best done when you have a specific problem to solve or a specific question to be answered. For instance, a specific question may be, *how can we eradicate COVID-19 from the world*. So, imagination is not about you just sitting down to fantasise, it is focused on the problem. And the problem will be specific. How do we eradicate poverty? How do we eradicate cancer? Your imagination should look for how you can find a solution. That is why it's called solution-driven.

THE PROCESS OF IMAGINATION

Imagination is an elaboration of an idea. It is the ability to fully develop an initial idea. An Idea is just like a single dot on paper, but imagination is expanding the idea, developing it, extrapolating it, and expanding it to a full concept. So what you do, in addition, is that you try to deconstruct the idea. Because ideas come as an indivisible whole. When you are trying to imagine around the idea, you're breaking down the idea. It is not cryptic or esoteric, it is what we do normally. You deconstruct the idea to break it down into functional parts, then you reassemble it again. That's what imagination is all about. You break it down and reassemble it. Deconstruct and reconstruct it.

To understand imagination, we need to understand how human beings or animals see. I will attempt to base the explanation of imagination on the human visual pathway. For me to see any object, light has to bounce on the object, then the object will reflect the light. Let's say I'm seeing my laptop now. Light is coming on my laptop, the light is being reflected into my eyes, it will pass through my lenses and go into my retina (retina is the photosensitive tissue at the back of your eye). So, that signal will be converted and pass through my optic nerve, from the optic nerve it will go to my thalamus from where it will be radiated to a point at the back of my head called the occipital lobe of your brain (We have the frontal lobe, parietal lobe, temporal lobe, and occipital lobe) On the occipital lobe, we have the visual pathway. So, it is the occipital lobe of the brain that houses the visual cortex.

The job of the visual cortex is to interpret the signal it receives. Before we see anything, our brain has to interpret it. Our brain gets the signal, the visual cortex processes it, the brain will then modify its splices and add some things, filling the gap. The visual cortex is divided into six parts (I'm adapting the structure of the visual cortex to teach about imagination) We have v1, v2, v3, v4, v 5, and v 6 parts of the visual cortex. Differentiation of the v1 is to interpret an object. So, when a signal gets to that v1, it only sees the object as lines and dots. If somebody is blind in v2, v3, v4, v5, and v6, but v1 is functioning well, what the person will see when he is looking at any object is dots and lines. The function of the v1 is to get the basic form of an image. V5 adds colour and motion to the object's colour. We call v2, v3, and v4 spatial orientation. This talks about how the object is located in space. They try to explain the location of objects in relation to other objects around.

The first step in imagination is constructing a basic form or a basic idea. The next step in imagination is transforming that basic idea or that basic form into an advanced, more elaborate form. The third step is when you begin to look at where and when. So, the first one is, what is it that we're trying to identify. Then, the next step is also what is it, but in an advanced form. And the third part focuses on what, where, and when?

To validate the visual cortex concept from the bible, let's see this account, 'Then He came to Bethsaida; and they brought a blind man to Him, and begged Him to touch him. So He took the blind man by the hand and led him out of the town. And when He had spit on his eyes and put His hands on him, He asked if he saw anything. And he looked up and said, "I see men like trees, walking." Then He put His hands on his eyes again and made him look up. And he was restored and saw everyone clearly'[24]

It means that initially when Jesus Christ touched this blind man, his v 1 and v 2 were completely healed. Remaining the v3, v4, v5, and v6. The Bible is so real. When the man said, 'I see men as trees' it meant that he was seeing lines and dots. In verse 25, Jesus Christ puts his hand on his eyes again and his sight was completely restored – colour and orientation were settled too.

When it comes to imagination, our ideas first appear like we are seeing men walking like trees. It will be blurry. Your ideas will sometimes appear confusing or vague. That's an idea that is not fully formed. Your imagination must go through that process – moving from confusion to clarity, from being vague to being clear.

So, your imagination goes through three main processes:

---

[24] Mark 8:22 -25 NKJV

1. One-Dimension: This is the basic form where all you see are lines and dots. So, you see in one-dimension only.
2. Two-Dimensions: Step two is the advanced form where you begin to add quality, shapes, features, and motion to your seeing. By the time you break an idea into two dimensions, you have gotten to the intermediate step.
3. Three-Dimensions: By the time we get to this step, we begin to look at the ways, space, and time of the idea. We are talking about the three dimensions.

When we receive an idea, it is usually very tiny, but within that idea is great potential. Using real-life situations to further drive home this point, let's consider architectural designs. When an architect designs a house, they go through the three steps we highlighted earlier. The first one is that they draw a schematic design. What I mean is that a general framework is designed to start with. Nobody starts with details because it can get you confused and tired. So, architects start with a general framework, then they move to more details which is step two. Then in step three, they begin to look at where this building will be situated or located in terms of space and in relation to other buildings around. After that, they go on to consider beauty.

Also, using the human body as an example, we have the major skeleton without which we can't stand. This comprises of the long bones in your body. These serve as the basic or general framework. Then for step two, we have what we call minor skeleton or small bones. In your hand, for instance, you have long bones, but in your wrist, or on your finger, you have numerous small bones. The last stage is to find out where one is located in space or in relation to order objects or human beings around.

Looking at a puzzle, how do you solve a puzzle? A puzzle is a big picture made up of small pieces. These small pieces are expected to be arranged to form that big picture. The best way to solve a puzzle is to, first of all, understand the basic pattern by taking a look at the big picture. You start by arranging the simple obvious basic pattern that jumps at you (step 1). You go on to settle the edges (step 2), then you move to the centre to finish the puzzle (step 3)

Now, let's look at music composition, it follows the same 3-step pattern. First of all, when you want to compose, you start from a basic tempo like one, two, three, four. You then move on to time signature or key signature. These are the foundation of good music. Time tempo, time signature, key signature – stage one. Next, you move to individual notes, adding voices, and instruments, that's stage two. At stage three, you decide where this music will be played. Is it in the cinema, or a concert? And then, when is it going to be played?

In visual arts (people that paint or graphic designers), a general outline is first established, they don't start with details. They paint the general outline first (stage 1), then they begin to add details and colour (stage 2). At stage three, they decide the kind of sculpturing they will do. Will they chisel out from wood, cement, or clay?

Finally, let's consider the idea of writing a book. I wanted to write a book about creativity that you are now reading. The first thing I did was to create a general framework for the book, that is, an outline explaining what I would be writing about. At stage two, I began to look at words, phrases, sentences, paragraphs, chapters, parts, etc. The first one is the conceptualization of the idea, which is the team. At stage three, I decided where the book was going to be published, how it would be published, and when it would be published.

THE CHILD OF IMAGINATION

After stage three of imagination, you have what I will call the child of imagination. What comes out of that imagination process? At least, after the third step of imagination, you are expected to have a clear vision and a workable plan. This is where you know if your imagination has been helpful, useful, or fruitful. You have a reproducible prototype or your pragmatic solution. The child of imagination is a prototype – a clear vision that is subject to improvement through a workable plan. Even for a workable plan, you still have to modify it as you go along.

DOCUMENTATION OF IMAGINATION

You must document your imagination. Whether you put it on software like a Dropbox paper or Microsoft word, or you pick a physical paper, or you get a diary and write it down. Documentation is an integral part of imagination and imagination is not complete without it. Documentation reinforces your imagination. Because as you imagine and write down, the movement of your hand, activates a part of your brain called the motor cortex.

The documentation process reinforces imagination, it helps you with your project. So, actively imagine by writing it down. Apart from the fact that it reinforces your imagination, it also improves your understanding of what you imagine, because if you can write something down and explain it, it's proof that you understand it. The more you can explain a concept or explain an idea, the more you can prove that you understand it and the more you understand it. Understanding is very important in creativity. Now, documentation also helps with record-keeping and memory recall because we practically forget, within one or two minutes, about fifty percent of what we hear. That is just part of human nature. Documentation also helps you to pass your message across to other people. When you are imagining, don't just use words. You can write words down, but above words, use symbols and shapes. I want to recommend that. Use symbols like arrows, triangles, circles, squares, graphs, pie charts, bar graphs, etc. Use them because communication is symbolic.

Let's establish a biblical foundation for documentation, 'I will stand my watch And set myself on the rampart, and watch to see what He will say to me, And I will answer when I am corrected. Then the LORD answered me and said: "Write the vision And make it plain on tablets, That he may run who reads it"'.[25]

Don't just sit down and receive ideas. Don't just sit down and imagine. Write it down! Write the idea down so that anyone who sees it can run with it. Seeing what you have written down will help you run with the idea yourself sometime later when you no longer feel up to it.

LIMITATIONS AND PITFALLS OF IMAGINATION

1. **Don't confuse imagination with hallucination**. Hallucination is a mental health condition. It is a sickness, a mental sickness. Once somebody has that he needs medical attention. But, how do you differentiate what you are imagining in terms of concept development or providing a solution to issues in the world to hallucination? Imagination is voluntary. What this means is that you are voluntarily doing what you are doing. Hence, if you don't want to imagine if you want to go and eat, you can stand up and eat or do any other thing. It is a voluntary

---

[25] Habakkuk 2:1-2 NKJV

process. It is controllable, while hallucination is involuntary, it's intrusive. Imagination is not intrusive. You have will over it while hallucination isn't. Visual hallucination is not controllable. Imagination is controllable. Visual hallucination is sometimes unconscious, something that just happens, while imagination is a conscious process. Visual hallucination is distressing. Distressing because it is a pathologic thing. It is distressing to you, because you may be seeing something like animals pursuing you. Imagination is not distressing. It is enjoyable. Though you can have hallucinations that can be enjoyable too. Finally, hallucination is delusional. It is delusional and it's based on a false belief, while imagination is based on knowledge, fact, memory, or logic.

2. **Imagination is just an approximation**. It's a shadow of things to come. It is potential. It is an immature baby. A baby has the same parts as an adult, but not fully developed. So the product of imagination is just like an immature baby. A good dose of realism is needed. Don't say because you have imagined something (e.g. You imagine that you are going to have a very big

veterinary practice) you are just going to jump and start doing things. No, that is immaturity. Just know that it is only a shadow of a potential that needs to be fully developed. I need to interact with other concepts in the world. You need to situate it in the light of what is happening around the world. For instance, there are some businesses that you can start now that will make you lose your money. If you go and start a talk show during COVID-19 (when this book was written), nobody is going to come to your talk show. Because in fact, there is a policy that people should not gather up more than 20 in a place. So it may be a brilliant idea, brilliant imagination, but if you are not realistic about it, you will just go and invest your money or your resources into something that is not beneficial.

If you want to start, what else do you want to start? Just look at anything. If you want to start an importation business, you want to import things into Australia, this is not the time to start. You may have a beautiful idea, you know, if you go and put your money in it, you will be making an unwise decision. People are not accepting goods from China again at the moment. So, this is not the time to venture into such.

3. Imagination is limited. Limited in the sense that you don't limit God within the confines or boundary of your imagination. The Bible says God is able to do much more than we can ever think or imagine[26]. So, you cannot possibly imagine all the possibilities. I am saying that we need to make room for God to work out a miracle; for God to be God and human beings to be human beings. There is no amount of imagination that you do that will take you to the level of God And your imagination can never be more important than the instruction of God. If the instruction that God gives you contradicts your imagination, you drop that imagination and follow the instruction, not the other way around. In other words, don't allow your imagination to limit God. Give God room knowing that your imagination can never be complete.

4. **Avoid pride**. Remember the people who wanted to build the tower of Babel, it was pride that wrecked them. They wanted to make a

---

[26] Ephesians 3:20

name for themselves. And the reason why God punished the people is that they never retained Him in their imagination. So, avoid pride because when you begin to see possibilities; I can do this thing, pride can set in. You need to be very careful. Imagination is very important. And God was the first person to imagine thereby encouraging us to imagine. Everybody imagines. God imagines. Satan imagines. Demons imagine. Angels imagine. But look at the example of Satan. Satan said, 'I will ascend into heaven, I will exalt my throne above the stars of God; I will also sit on the mount of the congregation On the farthest sides of the north;'[27] He had not done it but was just imagining himself upon the throne of God. But God said, 'At this level of imagination, you will never complete that process. I'm going to cast you down.' Jesus Christ said, 'I saw Satan fall like lightning from heaven'[28] So, be careful of pride. Let God be God.

---

[27] Isaiah 14:13 NKJV
[28] Luke 10:18 NKJV

4

EMOTIONS

In this chapter, we're going to look at the role of emotions in imagination and creativity. It is so integral to the process of creativity. Without emotion, it would be very hard to create anything or to achieve anything in life. Therefore, we must understand emotions and the roles they play in creativity and be able to harness the power of emotion to do something. Emotion is a summation of your subjective feelings per time. So, it's a mixture of our subjective feelings. The keyword here is feeling or feelings. How you feel per time is a summative average in the sense that you could be feeling happy at the same time, you can be feeling angry. Yes. It's possible to feel several emotions at the same time. As a son, you may be feeling secure at this moment because you are your father's son. As a partner, you may be happy and feeling jealous because your partner is somewhere. A student may be feeling anxious because of an exam coming in the next two weeks. This is why I say it's a summative average of your subjective feeling at a particular time.

What that means is that if the time changes, maybe in the nights, feelings can change. Your emotion can change at a particular place. Your feelings may change in terms of your subjective feeling about a particular thing. The way I feel about money is different from the way I feel about work. The way I feel about the blue colour may be different from the way I feel about the black colour. Emotions are more than feelings, but for this book, let's say emotions are just feelings.

Positive emotions enhance creativity while a negative emotion can disable it. Emotions affect your creativity, your performance on a job, etc. Whether you will pass an exam or not, or whether you will be successful in any project or not is a function of how you feel. We cannot run away from our emotions. The best thing we can do is understand them. I have selected 10 emotions that you should understand or utilise; how to generate, enhance, puppet, reproduce or multiply them.

1. PLEASURE

It is a feeling of satisfaction. When you do something that you feel satisfied with, it gives you a sense of pleasure. It pleases you. The project you are working on, the company you want to build, the book you want to write, the house you want to build, the marriage you want to build, or anything you want to create; once you think about that thing, it should give you a pleasurable feeling. The reason for this is that, by design, human beings pull away from anything painful. We want to experience periodic pleasurable experiences. The more pleasurable the feeling you have about your project, the easier for you to achieve it. Now let's look at an example in the Bible. Every time God created something during the creation of the earth, it was pleasing to Him. That's the feeling you must have in anything you are trying to create, or you are creating, or you're about to create. Pleasure can also mean the feeling you have after eating a good meal, drinking cold water or soft drink after a long period of thirst, the climax during sexual intercourse with your spouse, etc.

2. HAPPINESS

Happiness is also good. We call it anything that you think about that makes you happy. You feel happy when there's something good happening; when you have loads of dollars in your bank account, when you pass an exam, etc. It's also called excitement or cheerfulness, similar to joy. And that's why the Bible said that the joy of the Lord is our strength[29]. Joy or happiness happens when something good happens or in anticipation of something good that's likely to happen, like the feelings that come with a woman who got pregnant after five years of waiting.

3. GRATITUDE.

When somebody gives something to you that you didn't work for, or you didn't deserve, you are often grateful. For instance, you didn't work for it, but I gave you $10,000, that feeling of being grateful or being thankful, or having a sense of being privileged or special, is called gratitude. By nature, we are more grateful when we are given things that we didn't expect or are not qualified for.

---

[29] Nehemiah 8:10

4. **PEACE.**

Peace is also important in creativity. That's why the Bible says you should pursue peace with all people[30] God wants us to be peaceful for our own sake. Peace is a feeling of ease, tranquility, or calm. It's a feeling of relief, bliss, kindness, that sense of calmness around you. It's very encouraging. It helps you. It's not complacency. That's why every country that is relatively more is more creative. This is the reason why the Western world is relatively more peaceful than Africa. If there is war in your country, you'd be talking about survival. You don't even have time for creativity. God wants us to be at peace with all men, not only for our health benefits, or the peace of the world, or interpersonal relationships but also for creativity.

5. **LOVE**

No, I'm not talking about the technical definition of love here. I'm talking about the feeling aspect of love or the romantic feeling. That feeling that you have when somebody shows affection or your partner shows romantic love to you. That feeling you have as a result is what we call the feeling of love. Imagine that you are thinking about your partner, and you're feeling

---

[30] Hebrews 12:14

romantic and feeling loved, don't let it go to waste. Transfer that feeling into a project, or something right.

6. HOPE

When you have hope, you're expecting the future to be better. You expect your future, project, or life generally to get better. You're expecting something good. Hope is an expectation of something good. When you have something to live for, it's called aspiration or anticipation, expectation, optimism, or inspiration. If I promise you that I'm going to give you a thousand dollars in the next week, by default you become creative. You've not even gotten the money, it is not yet in your account, but the fact that you trust that Paul is going to give you the money, you're going to be creating things; whether you want to invest it, or buy a car, and so on. That expectation is hope. We should be hopeful. That hope is very important.

7. CONFIDENCE

This is also important. The feeling of confidence. I'm not talking about the act of confidence. No, we are dealing with feeling the feeling of confidence. When you are feeling confident about anything, you are more likely to push yourself. Of course, you need competence. You need to know how much more you know. So, you feel confident when you can do something, or you are prepared very well to do something. When you feel secure, that is confidence. And this confidence has so much to do with your outer confidence. It has so much to do with your intelligence and your creativity. If you are not confident, nobody will know it. You may be in a class where a question is asked by the teacher and you know the answer, but because you are not confident, then you're not going to raise your hand and nobody will know that you know it. So do not cast away your confidence because has great reward[31] Confidence is a good pride. A healthy self-pride or good self-esteem is good for you.

8. **PASSION**.

Passion is drive; that feeling that you have to do what you love to do. It's that feeling that you have when you get enthusiastic about something. When you are fanatic about what you want to create; the music you want to create, the book you want to write, or whatever piques your interest. It's your motivation for doing something. It also gets you curious. For instance, I am passionate about football, and I particularly love Chelsea football club and Mourinho (as a coach)

---

[31] Hebrews 10:35

9. TRUST

Feeling of trust is the feeling you have that somebody cannot disappoint you. It's very dangerous to have a relationship where there's so much mistrust and suspicion around. This will drain your creative energy. It's best that you leave any relationship where you don't trust the people involved. That feeling of reliance you have that someone will be loyal to you or protect you, like the feeling you have towards your parents, is trust. This feeling of trust is very key to creativity.

10. PURPOSEFULNESS OR DIRECTION.

That feeling you have when you want to do something for a good purpose. When you have that sense of direction, the feeling you have is core purposefulness. It also comes when you are contributing something positive to humanity or contributing something to the team. It is called a sense of purpose which can make you do more and make you more creative and intelligent. We can easily take the initiative when we are doing something purposeful.

HOW TO GENERATE POSITIVE EMOTIONS

Now, how do we generate positive emotions? Positive emotions are intertwined. One can lead to the other. Confidence and passion can result in love and gratitude. Peace can lead to trust, and so on. Below are some ways you can generate positive emotions:

1. Read the bible

As a Christian, the Bible is not just any kind of book. It's a book of intelligence. The book is a *cheat book* for life. Whenever you are feeling discouraged, pick up the promises of God for your life. And that's one of the reasons why we should read the Bible. The Bible exposes you to the good plans that God has for you and this creates positive emotions. Where it says that God loves you, you feel that love. Where God said He will never leave you or forsake you, it creates a sense of trust and confidence in you. The Bible is full of God's promises (from Genesis to Revelation) that you can use to generate positive emotions.

'This Book of the Law shall not depart from your mouth, but you shall meditate in it day and night, that you may observe to do according to all that is written in it. For then you will make your way prosperous, and then you will have good success'[32] When you focus on the positive things that the Word of God contains, you will be encouraged.

2. Harness your past victories.

If you are feeling a lack of commitment or not feeling confident, go to your past and see those times that you have been successful. The times you made the right decisions, when you made the right investment, the first book you wrote, the first exam you passed, and so on. Go back to them. That was what David did when he faced Goliath, he remembered how he had killed the lion and bear[33] which built his emotional confidence.

3. Creative environment.

I have this room where I have books stacked. Anytime I need to reference anything, I easily reach out to them. This room is a creative room for me. It's my library and my room of creativity. I painted the room white, pink, and blue because I love white, pink, and blue colours. It's a big room. I chose those colours to help activate my creativity. Sometimes, I want silence, so I just go into the room. You need to have a creative room too whose ambience helps you to be creative. Spice up the

---

[32] Joshua 1:8 NKJV
[33] 1 Samuel 17:33-37

room with colours, objects, music, or anything that will help you to be creative. Certain music can generate the different kinds of positive emotions I discussed earlier.

4. **Social interaction with creative people or positive-minded people**.

You are your friends. You become who your friends are. Do more with creative people. They, by default, will rub off their creativity on you. If you move with positive-minded people, people that are optimistic about life, they will influence you positively. Social interaction is very important. There's a limit to what I can do alone in my room. But by the time I go to walk or go to church or go to my best friend, I get rejuvenated. If you are looking for ideas, if you want to be more strategic, try to grab from people who already have these. Distance yourself from negative people. When you are feeling down or depressed, you can pick up motivational books or inspirational books or videos and audios.

5. **Forgiveness**

Forgiveness is beyond Christianity or religion. If you love yourself, if you want to achieve your highest potential in life, if you want to create things, then Forgive people. Forgiveness is something that can open up your brain. Forgiveness is giving. Forgive quickly to help you in your creativity. Unforgiveness will take up your creative space.

NEGATIVE EMOTIONS OR DISABLING EMOTIONS

Negative emotions are like too much load on your head. You cannot walk freely. They make you feel uncomfortable. You need to know how to deal with pain and how to even utilise it creatively.

1. DISPLEASURE

Displeasure is the opposite of pleasure. It is that feeling that you have when you are not satisfied with something. It usually comes as a result of an unpleasant event. Someone who has an injury will be displeased. Fun activity will be the last thing on such a person's mind. Bad news will also leave you displeased.

2. SADNESS

Sadness can mean depression or unhappiness It drains your cognitive capacity. It is the opposite of happiness and related to displeasure.

3. INGRATITUDE

Ingratitude drains you of creative power, creative ability. It happens when you're ungrateful for what God has given to you.

4. ANXIETY

Anxiety is worrying about the future e.g. lack of resources for what you're not supposed to do. Anxiety takes a large real estate in your brain. So it is an enemy of creativity.

5. HATRED

When you dislike somebody you can kill yourself, it can eat you up. It drains you of your creative power.

6. HOPELESSNESS

This is an abandonment of hope. It's a state where someone gives up on his future or dream. You need to know how to deal with it because it can destroy your power or sense of creativity.

7. TIMIDITY

Everybody has doubts. People that succeed act despite their self-doubt. Anytime I have to preach, I don't have a hundred percent confidence. God has not given us a spirit of timidity. Anybody that has a spirit of timidity cannot exercise faith and faith is very important in creativity. Believe that God has given you the capacity to do what He has asked you to do. You must believe that God has given you and you have it. Don't be like Gideon that kept saying he was the smallest. Timidity should not be mistaken for humility. Be courageous.

8. APATHY

Own your idea. It's your inheritance. Complacency can make you mediocre

9. MISTRUST

Mistrust can drain you of your creative power because if you cannot trust people, no one will be able to watch out for your interest or cover your back. You need people to believe in your idea and push your course.

10. PURPOSELESSNESS

Another thing that you should avoid is a lack of direction. When you have this feeling that you're lacking direction, it is a very bad thing that can drain you because you're not going anywhere. So, you're not going to put your best foot forward or put your best effort into the project.

HOW TO TURN NEGATIVE EMOTIONS AROUND

Now let's look at how to deal with negative emotions in the context of creativity. Negative emotions can be beneficial. Emotions are like energy and according to Physics, energy cannot be destroyed, it can only be transferred from one form to another. You cannot destroy that negative emotion. You can only convert or transfer it.

Transfer of Aggression

Imagine somebody did something wrong to you. You will feel angry and you are likely to transfer that negative emotion to others. It is called the transfer of aggression. But instead of transferring that negative emotion to others who don't even know what happened, you can transfer that emotion to something positive.

Reframing

You can reframe your emotion. Now, you may be feeling so pissed off, breathing heavily, you can tell yourself that I am not feeling angry but feeling excited. You can convert that negative emotional energy to positive emotional energy.

Accept It and Work with It

If you cannot transfer it, then accept it and do what you have to do. You may lose $10,000 in an investment and you feel so bad that you don't want to invest again. You need to accept that it has happened and don't allow it to stop you from moving forward.

Physical Exercise

Whenever you have any negative emotion, get out into the community and go exercise.

Change Your Posture

You can change your posture physically to counteract your negative emotions per time.

5

SPEECH

Speech is the fourth stage of creation. However, it is the first phase that has a physical impact on the world. For instance, you may have an idea in your mind, but it doesn't impact others until you speak it out. Speech is a mini action. Once you begin to speak about an idea, you begin to initiate the action.

To create anything in this life, it must involve speech, whether written or spoken. Speech has creative power. Jesus said that the words I speak to you are spirits and life[34] In one place He spoke to the storm, *peace be still*. In another place, he cursed a tree and it died. Elijah

---

[34] John 6:63

called down fire upon the sacrifice in a power contest with the prophets of Baal. Ezekiel prophesied to dry bones. You also can speak to create your world.

The words that come out from the mouth of a king is his authority, so as a king in your sphere of existence, your words have power.

The Operations of Speech

1. Speech directed upward: This is a speech directed to God. When you receive an idea, you need to use your mouth to praise the giver of that idea first - God. Let the people praise you and the earth will yield its increase[35]. Praise is a catalyst. When you praise God, a creative process is activated.

Secondly, ask God for specific things; favour, angelic support, nature cooperation, etc. over your idea or project. Ask and you shall receive[36]

2. Speech directed inward: This is positive, affirmative, self-talk, especially in your closet. You go into the Word of God and speak the scriptures that talk about your project, or a particular need at the moment. You meditate loudly and confess the Word of God. Your project, creative idea, can never rise above your

---

[35] Psalms 67:6
[36] Mathew 7:7

declaration. It becomes what you call it. Because whatever you say, you eventually believe, and whatever you believe, you eventually act out. If God has exalted His Word above His name, and cannot rise above His word, you also cannot rise above your word. Overcome by the word of your testimony.

3. **Speech directed towards nature**: Nature was created for you to dominate[37]. Kings dominate by decrees (words). Hence, you can command nature and its laws to align positively towards you. Like Moses parted the red sea with the rod (significant of the tongue), you can part obstacles before you. For instance, you can command resources e.g. money to serve you. Governmental barriers, social barriers, etc. can be brought down by the power of your speech. You can also command demons, who are also creations of God, to bow to the name of Jesus.

4. **Speech directed towards people**: You can use your speech to get things done socially. It is within the social space that your resources, inheritance, ideas, etc. find expression. Strategically use your speech to get involved and build in the social environment. Remember that the tower of Babel project was destroyed by God, indirectly, by destroying their social

---

[37] Genesis 1:27-28

language and social cohesion. This was simply because the project was not sanctioned by God. Use your words to approach family, friends, colleagues, investors, etc. about your project. 'Now the children of Israel had done according to the word of Moses, and they had asked from the Egyptians articles of silver, articles of gold, and clothing. And the LORD had given the people favor in the sight of the Egyptians, so that they granted them what they requested. Thus they plundered the Egyptians.'[38]

Your project is your promised land. Asking people is part of the creative process. After asking for favour from God, you can go ahead to ask for the favour of the people. Use your mouth to ask for money, favour, ideas, connections, secrets, etc. The things you need to execute your projects are already here on earth in the hands of your family, friends, neighbours, etc. Market and advertise your ideas. Marketing and advertising are based on speech which initiates creation. Be conscious about the word you release, whether by text or speech.

5. **Speech directed at your idea/project**: Whatever you are trying to build (e.g. a phone manufacturing company), you have to call it by name just like a living

---

[38] Exodus 12:35-36NKJV

thing. God calls those things that be not as though they exist[39]. You need to call the project or idea into being like you will speak to your child. The way Peter spoke to that lame man at the beautiful gate to rise and walk[40] is the same way you should speak to your project to rise and walk. Also, Jesus called Lazarus to come out from the grave[41], that's the same way you can call your project out of deadness or inactivity so that it will benefit you and benefit the world at large. Ezekiel also spoke to the dry bones and they became a mighty army[42].

[39]Romans 4:17
[40] Acts 3:6
[41] John 11:43
[42] Ezekiel 37:10

6

ACTION

This is where the rubber meets the road. It is where most of us give up. Action is work. This physical world is that of activities where everything is moving, even in your body. Hormones, enzymes, etc. are moving in your body. According to the Jews, there are four worlds; illumination, creation, formation, and action. To understand the action phase of the creative process, we must understand the concept of work or labour. Speech is easy, anybody can talk, but you must work. Action is work. After you have received the idea, confirmed it is from God, imagined it, felt good about it, and spoke to it, you need to go ahead and act. Laziness is not allowed in this phase. You must be willing to do the work. Paul told Timothy to do the work of an Evangelist. For anything to come to reality, work must be done. That is, you must overcome resistance. Of course, we have the grace of God to help us, but things won't just fall in place without work on our path. Many Christians are guilty of this. They keep waiting when they are meant to be acting. Embrace and enjoy work. There is dignity in labour. You can do smart hard work.

THE CONCEPT OF WORK.

God was the first person to work. Work started before we came to the world. Work didn't come after the fall of man. It started before the fall. Great men of faith in the bible had to embrace work. Let's look at a few of them:

1. ADAM

"This is the history of the heavens and the earth when they were created, in the day that the LORD God made the earth and the heavens, before any plant of the field was in the earth and before any herb of the field had grown. For the LORD God had not caused it to rain on the earth, and there was no man to till the ground; but a mist went up from the earth and watered the whole face of the ground. And the LORD God formed man of the dust of the ground and breathed into his nostrils the breath of life, and man became a living being'[43]

Initially, there was no man to do the work of tilling the ground, so God had to get his hands dirty by making man from the ground. The work phase is the actual phase of moulding and building.

'Then the LORD God took the man and put him in the garden of Eden to tend and keep it'[44] Adam was created to work.

2. NOAH

'And Noah began to be a farmer, and he planted a vineyard'[45] Noah worked as a farmer after the flood that destroyed the whole earth then preserving only his family.

3. ENOCH

Enoch walked with God and he was not for God took him. Some Jewish accounts believe that apart from Enoch being a man of God, he was also a shoemaker. Our Fathers of faith worked. It's a bad thing to expect that without work we will get the things we need.

---

[43] Genesis 2:4-7 NKJV
[44] Genesis 2:15 NKJV
[45] Genesis 9:20 NKJV

4. NIMROD

'Cush begot Nimrod; he began to be a mighty one on the earth. He was a mighty hunter before the LORD; therefore it is said, "Like Nimrod the mighty hunter before the LORD." And the beginning of his kingdom was Babel, Erech, Accad, and Calneh, in the land of Shinar. From that land he went to Assyria and built Nineveh, Rehoboth Ir, Calah, and Resen between Nineveh and Calah (that is the principal city).'[46]

Before these verses, there was no mention of a mighty man upon the earth. And what made Nimrod mighty was the work of his hand - hunting. Hunting was his profession. He had to get involved in his work and labour. It's interesting to note that the phrase, 'before the Lord' was added after the mighty hunter. This is to show that God validates work. If God attaches His name to you, it means He approves your actions. Reference is also made to Nimrod building. That means he was a hunter and builder. God wants us to be builders. Your labour or work is a building effort. It's easier said than done, though. Nimrod was both a mighty man and a hunter for God.

---

[46] Genesis 10:8-12 NKJV

5. ABRAHAM AND ISAAC

Abraham was the father of faith. He was the personality that introduced us to faith walk with God. He was into husbandry. Showing us that a faith-building person must embrace the concept of work. There is a difference between work and toiling. Toiling is a curse, but work is a blessing. When you toil, you work without anything to show for it. It is fruitless labour and unproductive work.

'Then to Adam He said, Because you have heeded the voice of your wife, and have eaten from the tree of which I commanded you saying, 'You shall not eat of it': Cursed is the ground for your sake; in toil you shall eat of it All the days of your life. Both thorns and thistles it shall bring forth for you, And you shall eat the herb of the field. In the sweat of your face you shall eat bread Till you return to the ground, For out of it you were taken; For dust you are, And to dust you shall return.'[47]

Toiling happens when you overwork but get underpaid. Isaac was a farmer. Abraham and Isaac were workers. In fact, their concept of faith was in the context of their secular work - their experience outside

---

[47] Genesis 3:17-19 NKJV

their spiritual work. The concept of faith that we have today is often limited to the church or spiritual things. For them, it extended to their community and work. If God is faithful, they wanted to see that faithfulness demonstrated on their farm. If God is mighty, they wanted to see that demonstrated in their hunting.

6. JACOB

It was in the place of Jacob working for Laban that God gave him a brilliant idea. God gave him that idea while he was tending Laban's sheep. Note that this idea came in relation to what he was already doing. If Jacob was lazy, he wouldn't have received that idea. If it wasn't already his line of work and he received such an idea, he wouldn't have understood it.

7. JOSEPH

Whatever Joseph did prospered, even when he was in prison. He embraced the concept of work everywhere he was and did well.

8. MOSES

God called Moses when the work he was doing was tending his father-in-law's sheep. He was already a busy man. God should find you busy when He calls you. Let Him find you already working. What this does for you is that when you already have the right work ethics, you will be able to transfer it to what God calls you unto. Moses wasn't an idle man. God doesn't call idle men. God promised the Israelites that He would bless the works of their hands. He is the One who gives us the power to make wealth. Hence, without work, there can't be blessing.

'Blessed shall you be in the city, and blessed shall you be in the country. Blessed shall be the fruit of your body, the produce of your ground and the increase of your herds, the increase of your cattle and the offspring of your flocks. Blessed shall be your basket and kneading bowl. Blessed shall you be when you come in, and blessed shall you be when you go out. The LORD will cause your enemies who rise against you to be defeated before your face; they shall come out against you one way and flee before you seven ways. The LORD will command the blessing on you in your storehouses and in all to which you set your hand, and He will bless you in the land which the Lord your God is giving you.'[48]

The blessing and increase can only come as by-products of your work.

---

[48] Deuteronomy 28:3-8 NKJV

9. GIDEON

Gideon was at the threshing floor when God came to him through the angel and gave him the assignment of defeating the Midianites that had been oppressing them.

10. DAVID

God called David while he was a shepherd. And to be a shepherd in those days was a big business. David was working for his father as a shepherd, and he transferred that skill into what he eventually did for God.

11. ELISHA

Elijah called Elisha while he was plowing with the oxen.

'So he departed from there, and found Elisha the son of Shaphat, who was plowing with twelve yoke of oxen before him, and he with the twelfth. Then Elijah passed by him and threw his mantle on him. And he left the oxen, and ran after Elijah, and said, "Please let me kiss my father and my mother, and then I will follow you. And he said to him, "Go back again, for what have I done to you?"'[49]

---

[49] 1 Kings 19:19-20 NKJV

All these strong men of God embraced the concept of work and we must embrace the concept of work too. Jesus Christ was a carpenter. He learnt the trade of His earthly father - Joseph. In another place, He said that He must do the work of His (heavenly) Father[50]. He also taught with many parables like the parable of the sower, the parable of talents, etc. to underscore and validate the concept of work. Peter was a fisherman, and that was what he returned to when Jesus died. Paul was a lawyer and a tentmaker. All these people understood work ethic. They understood that your work is your inheritance and dignity. When you take the organisation you want to build or profession as your God-given inheritance and dignity, then you have moved into the action phase of the creative work.

THE CONCEPT OF TIME AND SEASON.

You have an idea or project, but you must understand the concept of time and season. For instance, if you love to plan events, the season of COVID-19 is the wrong time to want to put up an event just because you have the idea. The global pandemic necessitated that many countries shut down activities. Going against

---

[50] John 9:4

such a governmental directive can get you arrested. You need to understand the season to get things done.

Let me share my example. When I felt called into ministry and wanted to start immediately, I went to someone to seek counsel and I was advised to calm down and allow time to prove it. I went back to God and discovered that the season had changed when it comes to how ministry is done these days. It was in 2018 I started having ZOOM meetings. I realised then that there was going to be a shift in the way people do ministry. Of course, I understand the place of physical meetings.

UNDERSTAND YOUR ENVIRONMENT

Also, you need to understand your environment. It is good to want to take massive action and work on your idea, but it is also very important to work in an environment that is conducive to your idea. No matter how hard you work, some ideas will not work in certain environments, just like certain seeds will not grow in certain soils or environments no matter how much you try. Certain ideas may thrive in Nigeria or other third world countries that will never thrive in the western world.

START WHERE YOU ARE

Having stressed the importance of time and season as well as the environment, I must also mention that you need to learn to start from where you are. Don't wait until you have a 100 percent conducive environment. This may sound contrary to what I stated earlier about the environment. As much as you want the environment to be right, you must learn to start from where you are. You must start where you are with what you have. After God had called Gideon for a great and seemingly impossible task, Gideon came up with excuses why he wasn't fit for the job, but God told him to, *'Go in this your might'* Go in this your might, in your case, may mean start with what is in your hand. You may need 10 million dollars for a business, but all you now have is 100, 000 dollars, why not see what you can do by starting with that 100, 000 dollars that you have? There will never be a perfect time to start.

CONFIDENCE

When you get to the action phase, you must be confident. Confidence brings reward. Don't cast away your confidence. Therefore do not cast away your confidence, which has great reward[51]. It is your confidence that will bring you a reward in your idea generation and project execution. We see this confidence exemplified by Jesus Christ. We see Jesus using the principle of 'I am' a lot in the Bible. This was not an exhibition of pride, but an expression of holy confidence. You should be able to see the idea that God has given you as your inheritance – something that God has given you that you should be proud of. You must embrace the idea God has given you and own it. It may be to build the next Facebook or a global company. Nobody deserves that idea more than you. If God singled you out of over 7 billion people on earth to give that idea, then you should own it and pursue it with confidence, regardless of your age, gender, colour, country, etc.

SEE THE IDEA OR PROJECT AS A MORAL ISSUE

Is it sinful not to complete a project? Is it sinful to go back? If you are not able to pursue that project or idea to the last mark, it is a sin because sin means to miss the mark. If you see your project or idea as a moral or ethical issue, then you are most likely to see it through.

---

[51] Hebrews 10:35 NKJV

You will see the failure of the idea as a sin towards God like Joseph saw sleeping with Potiphar's wife as sin.

DEVELOPING YOUR SKILL AND COMPETENCE

Developing your skill and competence in the area of your idea is part of the action you must take. If God drops the idea to be a speaker into your heart and you can't speak well yet, you want to see to it that you develop your ability to communicate. If God told you to be the best pilot in the world and you don't know anything about flying, then you want to go to the best aviation school to go and learn how to fly a plane.

DEVELOP A COMPETITIVE EDGE AROUND YOUR IDEA OR PRODUCT

There are three things I have discovered in my life as what gives an idea or product a competitive edge - comfort, speed, and reliability. If your idea or project can give comfort to people, speedily, and reliably then people will rush it. When you look at the idea you have, think of comfort, speed, and reliability. For instance, McDonald is a massive franchise when it comes to fast foods because it is comfortable. You don't have to go to the market to buy food items to cook.

Then they also sell speed. As soon as you drive in, within two minutes you have your food. Then they are reliable because you know that whenever you get to McDonald, you must get something to eat.

THE CONCEPT OF PATIENCE, CONSISTENCY, AND PERSEVERANCE

Patience is about time. Being able to stay long enough. Seeing an idea to its execution is a marathon. You need patience which also confirms your faith in God. Consistency is the ability to do something over and over. To be there always. Perseverance is needed when there is opposition. This is the ability to stay put when the conditions are not favourable, when there is so much going against you than for you.

FOCUS

Focus is about maintaining a target by avoiding distractions. Distractions are things that try to stop you from focusing on your goal. Let me use Microsoft as an example. I remember stumbling on Bill Gate's interview on television where he regretted missing out on the mobile phone market in the late 90s. He said Microsoft was well-positioned to dominate the mobile phone industry because they had the technology. All they needed to do at Microsoft was adapt their software for phones before the likes of android and other companies showed up. He said they were distracted by a lot of lawsuits in the US then. Distractions are usually challenges and other bad things that stop us from pursuing our goals.

Side attractions, on the other hand, are usually good things that prevent us from pursuing the best. For instance, you may want to start a big farming company. Side attraction to you may be an idea brought to you to start an IT company instead when what you should do is focus on starting the farming company. Your side attraction is usually the focus of another person.

You need to maintain your focus by avoiding distractions and side attractions on your journey.

FLEXIBILITY

You must be flexible with the generation of your ideas. Imagine the manufacturers of Mainframe computers, IBM rejecting Bill Gate's idea that eventually took over the world of computers. Flexibility is the ability to surrender biases and preconceptions. One of the major reasons for stagnancy in life is non-flexibility. Ideas don't always come as a full package, hence the need to be flexible with them through modification after exposure to more wisdom and feedback. Flexibility is the ability to adapt. There is a concept of Adaptation in Biology that explains that the species that survive are the ones that can adapt to their environment.

WHAT TO DO WHEN YOU ARE DISCOURAGED

Now, you are taking massive action, doing everything within your power to see your ideas come alive, I need you to understand that discouragement is part of the package. To say the journey will be easy is a lie. Expect resistance. Expect discouragement. If it is a massive project, there will be a time that you feel like giving up. We must learn to embrace failures and lessons that come with them as much as we embrace success. Failure is part of life.

Even Jesus got discouraged at the point of fulfilling His ultimate purpose when He realised the pain and suffering that awaited Him and He wished that the cup could pass over Him. Discouragement is part of the bargain. If you are not failing, you are not succeeding.

I love playing the game of chess and I have discovered that it is when I lose a game that I learn. If I play with a weak opponent and win with a margin like 7-0, I discovered that I don't learn anything. But when I play with a stronger opponent who beats me with a margin as wide as 10-0, I realised that I learn new things. You are meant to learn from your defeat. So, see life as a game of chess. See your ideas as a game of chess. You win some and lose some. What if the market rejects your idea? The market has no obligation to accept your idea no matter how lofty it appears to you or even if it is from God.

So, what do you do when you are discouraged? What do you do when the forces against you are more than the forces with you? Great men in the Bible days were discouraged – Abraham, Isaac, Ezekiel, Jeremiah, Paul, etc. Discouragement will surely come and the following are the things you can do when it comes:

1. Replay the memories of your past victories: At a time, David was discouraged, but He encouraged himself in the Lord. Also, when David was taken to King Saul as the challenger of Goliath and he was being schooled on how unqualified he was to face such a giant, he quickly shared the testimonies of how he killed a bear and lion at different times when they came to attack his sheep. No past victory is too small to harness and leverage for today's challenge. It could be passing an exam, making

your first 100, 000 dollars, etc. You must bring those memories back to life.

2. Replay good comments or recommendations of people: This may be the good comments of your spouse, parents, colleagues, friends, etc. It could also be the feedback or recommendation of a client or customer after using your product or enjoying your service. This is a good way to generate massive positive emotions. We all want to feel good about ourselves and one way we achieve this is by the good things other people say about us.

3. Count your blessings: We are in an age where everything is fast and competitive, however, we have got to learn how to count our blessings. Be grateful for the privileges that you have that others don't have, instead of complaining about what you don't yet have. Count your blessings and name them one by one. Write them down if you have to.

4. Rest: Sometimes, you feel discouraged not because of any major failure, but because you are exhausted. You probably are pushing yourself hard without eating or resting well. When you feel tired, you will feel discouraged. You need to learn to take a rest. Elijah was once discouraged like that and he had to rest and

feed well which replenished him for the journey ahead of him[52] When you are replenished, you automatically get encouraged to move on.

5. Talk to someone: When you are feeling discouraged, you need to learn to talk to someone. It could be your spouse, friend, mentor, or anyone that has your best interest at heart.

6. Go for seminars or training: Your idea or project may not be taking shape like you want, which gets you discouraged, simply because you lack the know-how. Ideas don't operate in a vacuum. Through seminars and training, you get exposed to the right people and information that can boost your ideas.

7. Read, watch videos, or listen to audio related to your idea: Reading books, watching videos, and listening to audio related to your ideas can serve as great boosters for you. Something is igniting and encouraging about reading from, watching, or listening to others who have gone ahead of you.

8. Go into partnership: At times, the reason why you are discouraged about your ideas is that you are doing it alone. Nobody is contributing

---

[52] 1 Kings 17:3-7

to or supporting your ideas. You need to go into a healthy partnership. This is why big companies do mergers and acquisitions or joint ventures. You can't do it alone.

9. Join forums and interest groups: You need to travel with people who are going in the same direction as you.

10. Focus on the reward: Focus on the glory to come. For the joy set before Him, Jesus endured the cross and despised the shame[53] When you focus on your reward, discouragement will dissipate. Money can be a form of reward when you think about how much your dream company can turn over per year. Focusing on the reward can energise you.

11. Music, jokes, and travel: Listening to good music or jokes can lift the soul. A change of environment can also elevate the spirit. When it comes to good music, they could be secular or religious, as long as they have lyrics that can motivate or edify.

---

[53] Hebrews 12:2

7

PARTING WORD

In rounding off this book, I will love to draw your attention to certain things:

1. Avoid Pride: Even though we have considered how we are gods with the ability to create like God, we must realise that we cannot take the place of God. No amount of creativity or invention can equate us to God.

2. Partner with God: Like we saw earlier in the scripture Genesis 2:4-7, the ground must be softened before you can plough it for cultivation. In the same vein, you must soften the ground for your idea or project by partnering with God. God caused water to rise from the ground first, even though He could send rain from heaven. The way you partner

with God is through giving Him your tithe, your time, giving to the poor, homeless, sick, partnering with ministries, etc. Giving back to society is a spiritual thing to do. You must tie your idea to God.

3. Fasting and Prayer: There is the spiritual aspect of life that must be taken care of. The devil is your adversary. Godly ideas stimulate adversary and warfare. One way the devil attacks your idea is to create a negative, unfavourable environment around it. Remember how he took everything away from Job. Engaging in fasting and prayer is good for you to secure your ideas spiritually.

4. Don't intentionally destroy other people's ideas or products: You must be careful not to intentionally destroy other people's ideas or products to build yours. Don't shift boundaries to favour you. Don't steal other people's ideas either.

5. Pay your tax: Paying tax is both a civic and spiritual responsibility. Authorities are instituted and appointed by God. Even Jesus paid tax.

6. Obey the law of the land: If there is a law that is against your idea, you have to comply with the laws. Get the necessary licenses and permits for your business or ideas. Obey the laws of the land where you reside.